MY MIRACLE MARINE

THE STORY OF THREE-TIME PURPLE HEART RECIPIENT
LCPL. JOHN MCCLELLAN

BY
CONNIE MCCLELLAN

Divine Word Publishing
Columbia, Missouri

ISBN 978-0-9798762-0-2
Library of Congress Control Number: 2008901164

Published by
Divine Word Publishing
Columbia, MO 65202

Book cover concept by Connie McClellan

Book cover layout and design, and interior layout and
design by Bookcovers.com

First Editor: Joan Rawson

Second Editor: Barri Bumgarner

Third Editor: Archer Ellison, Inc.

Acknowledgments

There are many to whom I wish to extend my gratitude for their contributions to the making of *My Miracle Marine*:

Most importantly, I thank God for his miraculous blessings & healings, without which there would no *My Miracle Marine*.

I thank my son, John, for allowing me to expose every detail of his being after September 26, 2006. Without his willingness for me to share all aspects of his experience and injuries, *My Miracle Marine* could not have been published.

I thank my husband, Carl for his patience and support during the writing of *My Miracle Marine*.

My deepest gratitude goes to Sgt. Mario Anes and all those who assisted in saving John's life on the battlefield in Iraq.

And, I am so grateful to all those who prayed and all those who continue to pray for John.

In addition, my heartfelt, everlasting appreciation goes to:

Angela Brittain, Brittain Communications for counsel, support and development of mymiraclemarine.com.

Joan Rawson, friend and editor, for the first editing.

Barri Bumgartner, author and editor, for the second editing.

John Bell, Ovid Bell Press for invaluable counsel.

All who allowed me to share their emails that we received during John's recovery.

www.mymiraclemarine.com

Contents

Foreword

God has many ways of showing Himself in our lives. Repeatedly, while our family endured the "experience" described in *My Miracle Marine*, God demonstrated that He is real, that He is with us every minute of every day, and that He is still in the business of working miracles.

During the months following our son, John's Iraq injury, time after time, we experienced small coincidental happenstances. Due to the frequency of these coincidences, it didn't take me long to recognize that they were from God. It was as though God  supernaturally wrapped His arms around us, assuring us, "I'm still here; I will not leave you or forsake you."

From the moment we learned of John's head injury, one by one, God miraculously answered our unceasing, faithful prayer requests. Some answers were awarded the same day, some the next day, some days later, some weeks or months later, and some are still in the works.

With the nature and extent of John's injuries, God's miracle working power is the only explanation for John's survival, and subsequent, recovery. We continue to pray and believe that God has a tremendous plan for John's life, that John is still God's work in progress and that God will ultimately restore John's mind and body to full health and strength.

viii

1

September, 2006

At midnight on September 26, 2006, the phone rang in our Columbia, Missouri home. Little did I know, this call would be the beginning of an emotional and spiritual journey that would change our lives...forever. Normally, when Carl and I received late night calls, we were excited because the calls were usually from our son, John, a Lance Corporal in the Marine Corps. John, a machine gunner stationed in Haditha, Iraq, was nine hours ahead of Missouri, which meant his days were our nights. Consequently, we expected and hoped for those late night calls.

I excitedly answered the phone, "Hello?" There was a hesitation on the other end, which is routine for overseas calls. I anticipated and said, "John, is that you? John?"

A man's voice inquired, "Mrs. McClellan?"

I hesitated, "Yes?"

"My name is Sgt. Hickem; I'm calling from Balad

Hospital in Balad, Iraq."

"Yes?" I felt the blood draining from my face, as my heart stuck in my throat.

"I regret to inform you…" *Oh my God, this can't be happening!* "Your son has been injured."

So relieved he didn't tell me John had been killed, for a brief second, my heart leapt for joy. *"Injured! Injured! We can do injured!"* Sadly, as the conversation continued, Sgt. Hickem expounded on how critically injured John was.

While on patrol with his unit, checking for roadside bombs, an enemy sniper made an expert shot, striking John in the head. The bullet penetrated just below his protective helmet, in front of his left ear and exited the back of his head in the lower, left quadrant. While his father and I slept, we were totally oblivious to the five hours of lifesaving surgery John had just endured. Sgt. Hickem informed us that the doctors had removed bone fragments and brain tissue, and that the doctor who assisted in the surgery would call us in an hour to give us more details on John's condition.

Carl, upon hearing my end of the initial conversation, immediately picked up the extension to hear the remainder of the conversation. After we hung up our respective phones, we cried and held each other for what seemed like hours, but may have only been minutes. We were mutually unable to converse, and, in retrospect, were clearly in a state of shock. Surreal was the only way to describe the moment. *This isn't happening...please tell me this isn't happening.*

One hour later, almost to the minute, we received a call from one of the doctors who assisted with John's surgery. "Mrs. Schneider?"

Praise God! They have John mixed up with someone else! This supported my initial denial.

Almost immediately, he corrected himself. "Oh, I'm sorry, I mean... Mrs. McClellan?

My heart sank. "Yes...?"

"My name is Dr. Hill. I assisted the neurosurgeon during John's surgery."

He continued, "John has sustained a very serious injury, and I'm sorry to relay that the prognosis is not good. If he survives the brain swelling, which is our biggest and most immediate concern, he will not be the same and...will more than likely be a vegetable. For the time being,however, he is stable."

Dr. Hill advised he would have the neurosurgeon give us a call in 24 hours to update us on John's condition. In the meantime, he advised that arrangements were being made to fly John to a military hospital in Landstuhl, Germany as soon as his condition would allow. His intracranial pressure had to stabilize before he could make the flight and even with that, the flight would be longer than normal, since with his vulnerability of elevated, intracranial pressure, the plane would have to fly at a very low altitude.

After hanging up the phone, with the word "vegetable" resounding in my head, I rushed to my computer to send an e-mail to everyone I could think of. Realizing the critical nature of the situation, I knew I had to rely on my prayer partners to begin praying for John as soon as possible. I had to put my hope in God, because at that moment, truly, that was the only hope I had. Little did I know that e-mail would be the first of over one-hundred-fifty that I would send over the course of the next twelve months.

From: Connie McClellan
Date: September 27, 2006 1:18 AM
Subject: Urgent prayers needed for John

It is with very heavy heart that I tell you that John has been seriously injured. He is being flown to a hospital in Germany. The prognosis is very bad. He was shot in the head by a sniper. The bullet went in by his ear and out his neck. No arteries were hit; however, brain tissue was removed in the surgery. At this point, we are hearing that if he lives, he will not be the same, and will more than likely be a vegetable. The only thing that can make him normal is a miracle from God. So, please pray with me:

Lord, we thank you that you are doing a miracle in John's mind and body. You have said in your Word, Lord, if we ask anything in your name that it will be done. We are asking, Lord, that you heal John, make him whole in every way, physically, mentally, spiritually, and emotionally. You are our only hope, God, in Jesus' name. Amen.

Please send this to everyone you know who believes
in prayer.
Thank you,
Connie

Carl and I resumed holding each other, still too
traumatized to speak. Finally, I returned to bed and
began praying as I had never prayed before. My mind,
in a state of shock, combined with the lack of sleep,
caused me to intermittently have to remind myself that
this was not a bad dream; this was real. As I lay there,
I encouraged myself by reflecting on how God and His
angels had protected John continuously over the past
two years. I prayed God's protection and mercy would
continue now by allowing John to live.

5

2

March, 2003

One afternoon, when John was a junior in high school, as I was folding laundry, the phone rang. The caller ID read *United States Government.*

Just two weeks prior, we had mailed our Federal income tax papers. *Crap, I don't have time for an audit.*

I answered hesitantly, "Hello?"

"Hello, Mrs. McClellan?"

"Yes?" anticipating who might be on the other end of the phone.

"This is Staff Sgt. Mulinax with the United States Marine Corps. I'm calling to respond to an inquiry from your son, John, about joining the Marines... is he there?"

Phew! Then, realizing what he just said, I exclaimed, "WHAT? You did... He did...*what?*"

We had no idea John was considering this. "I'll have him call you when he gets home."

About twenty minutes after I hung up the phone, John walked in the front door. I prodded, "John, I just received a call from the Marine recruiter. Have you applied to join the Marines?"

"I've made an inquiry about it."

"Are you seriously considering this?" My emotions were mixed. This could be a good thing for John in so many ways. Ideally, he could learn the discipline and structure we failed as parents to teach him. On the other hand, since the United States had just invaded Iraq, the future for a Marine would very uncertain, and the idea of him going to war had little appeal.

"Yeah, I've given it a lot of thought, and I really think this is what I want to do."

"Well, I've given it consideration for the past 20 minutes, and…this may not be a good time, but I think this might be a good thing for you."

Not only would joining the military teach John what he lacked, but it would also buy him time to determine what he wanted to do with his life. Even though he made good grades, school was not his thrust. He lacked the motivation and desire for college, which provided another reason for me to vote for the military as the initial career choice for John.

"Well, if I join now, it would be a year before boot camp. I really don't know what's going to happen over there between now and then, but… regardless…I don't have a problem going to fight for my country."

7

My eyes welled. "Oh, John, I'm so proud of you." I hugged him with a fierceness only a mother knows.

A month later, John joined the Marines under the "delayed entry" program. This would permit him to join as a Junior, thereby allowing him a credit of one year of inactive duty. Then, a year after enlistment, immediately after High School graduation, he would begin basic training.

3

June 2004

On June 5, 2004, John graduated from Columbia, Missouri's Hickman High School. On June 8, 2004, John, Carl and I met the recruiters and six young recruits at the Columbia Marine office. Carl and I watched as they all departed for the airport in the Marine van. Watching John wave from the van window stirred up similar emotions to the first day I put him on the school bus for kindergarten...magnified by no less than one hundred times. That evening John called from the Marine Corps Recruiting Depot (MCRD) in San Diego, California to tell us he had arrived and not to expect to hear from him for at least two months. *Two Months!?*

In September, 2004, John would be rewarded for his boot camp efforts with a graduation ceremony to be held at MCRD. Carl, my 87-year-old mother, my step-daughter, Jane, and I all flew to San Diego for the graduation ceremony and festivities. The anticipation

9

of the reunion was exhilarating for all of us, as we had not seen him in three months and had only spoken to him twice. When we arrived on base, hundreds of Marine recruits were jogging and running within the compound. We strained to pick John out of the masses. Quite frankly, they all looked alike – close cropped hair and lean. Finally, we saw him as he jogged by with his unit. My heart leapt as I recognized him. I can hardly remember a more proud parent moment. It was so exciting watching him and anticipating that first hug.

After the recruits finished their morning exercise, they showered, dressed and were then allowed to reunite with their families. What an incredible moment as we hugged after the graduation ceremony. He looked different...not just thinner...but more confident. It appeared that the last three months had become him.

John was allowed to leave the base for the remainder of an incredible weekend of fellowship for our family. I realized how, in the past, we had taken for granted our family time together. We let John decide what we should do with our time. He elected to spend time at the hotel rather than sightseeing or other available activities. The weekend culminated with the graduation ceremonies with all those boys in their uniforms. What a sight it was! After the ceremonies concluded, we returned to our hotel for the night, and the next morning, we all, including John, flew back to Missouri for his three week leave.

Three weeks later, John left Missouri for Kaneohe Bay, Hawaii, which had been designated as his home base. After seven months of training as a machine gunner at Kaneohe Bay, John deployed to Kunar Province in Afghanistan.

11

4

June, 2005

During John's deployment in Afghanistan, we learned that computer instant messaging would serve as our most effective form of communication. After much frustration with missed instant messages from John, I discovered that I could program my computer to ring through my cell phone as a text message whenever John would instant message us. It was exhilarating when we heard the unique, text message ring, as that meant John was online. At that point, Carl and I would immediately rush to a computer to converse. There were a number of times that I was in my car when I received the text message. I would frantically text message back, "Don't leave! I'll be home in ten minutes!" or whatever time I thought it would take. Often, I was at work where I didn't have instant messaging capability, so I would frantically call Carl to say, "Hurry! Hurry! John's online!" A number of times neither Carl nor I could get online in time and would miss connecting with him.

Those misses were heart-wrenching.

However, all in all, instant messaging worked perfectly, because after our conversation concluded, I would copy, paste, and e-mail the conversation to a group of approximately 100 people that I called my e-mail "entourage." This was beneficial for everyone as it kept them informed and interested, and gave them a taste of a "day in a life" of a Marine in Afghanistan. However, more importantly, it let them know exactly how to pray. I would preface each transmission with something similar to: "Please pray. Thank you, Lord, that you are protecting John and his buds every minute of every day, keeping them hydrated, nourished, comfortable and safe in Jesus' name. Amen." Or if there was a more specific prayer need, I would include that in the prayer. In this way, before my e-mail "entourage" could read the instant message, they would be prompted to pray for John and his comrades.

October 11, 2005 Instant Message
phil464me—me, MAC11222–John

Phil464me: hi

MAC11222: hows it going?

Phil464me: I'm so happy!! Your timing is PERFECT!! I was just getting ready to leave for work.

Phil464me: 1 minute more and you would have missed me! Phew!

MAC11222: good

Phil464me: How are U doing

MAC11222: dont freak out, but i got a purple heart today

Phil464me: What?!?!? WHY!? ? ?   HOW?!?!?

MAC11222: it was just a graze

Phil464me: Oh my gosh!!

Phil464me: How did it happen?

MAC11222: a little shrapnel grazed my wrist and my arm

Phil464me: Were you on the convoy?

MAC11222: we were on a convoy and got contact

Phil464me: Was it a bomb or an attack?

MAC11222: an attack

Phil464me: Thank you, Jesus, for the protection that you have given and continue to give john and ALL of his buds

Phil464me: So, are you in the hospital?

MAC11222: no

MAC11222: i didnt even need stitches

Phil464me: Thank you, Lord!!

Phil464me: So, did you get the people that shot you?

MAC11222: i fired back thats for sure

MAC11222: i just saw blood on my blouse and i just got mad and i couldnt even feel that i had got hit

Phil464me: Wow! You da Man!

MAC11222: i couldnt even really tell where it was coming from

MAC11222: yea if i had to get a purple heart this is the way i wanted to get it

Phil464me: Was anyone else hurt?

MAC11222: yea another guy got hit

MAC11222: but hes going to be ok

Phil464me: How bad was he hurt?

14

MAC11222: he took two rounds in the arm i think

Phil464me: bummer.........so, was it a grenade?

Phil464me: that hit you?

MAC11222: i think it was an rpg

MAC11222: shrapnel that got me

Phil464me: i c

MAC11222: i should be back in the gym in a couple days

Phil464me: excellent!

Phil464me: Be comforted in knowing that God's angels are all over you!!!

MAC11222: :)

Phil464me: I'm so grateful you're OK

Phil464me: So, when you get a purple heart, do they do a little ceremony? Or do they just give it to you when you're treated? Or, do they mail it to you, or what?

MAC11222: they have a ceremony

15

MAC11222: they had to cut my blouse to get my arm out of it

Phil464me: Have you been out on convoy today?

Phil464me: Was that when you got your injury?

MAC11222: ye

MAC11222: s

Phil464me: So, do they just put ointment on it and wrap it up?

MAC11222: thats all they needed to do

Phil464me: cool......thank you, Lord, for your protection of John and his buds every minute of every day, in Jesus' name, amen.

Phil464me: Sorry, if 'm being redundant.....lol

Phil464me: But the Bible says to pray without ceasing..... lol

Phil464me: Every morning when I'm on the eliptical,

Phil464me: the first thing I do is pray Psalm 91 over you.

Phil464me: I can feel God's presence with me, so I know he hears me and I KNOW, that I KNOW, that I KNOW that he is watching over you!!

MAC11222: :)

MAC11222: well, gtg, love you bye

Phil464me: I love you, too John. bye

OCTOBER 14, 2006

MAC11222: hey

Phil464me: hey

MAC11222: hows it going?

Phil464me: How R U?

MAC11222: good

MAC11222: i guess i still have a piece of shrapnel in my wrist

MAC11222: they are going to cut it out tomorrow

Phil464me: Oh my

Phil464me: How deep is it?

MAC11222: its like right on the surface

MAC11222: so its not to bad

Phil464me: Is it infected?

MAC11222: nope

Phil464me: Good deal.

MAC11222: Well, gtg, but I wanted to let you know what's going on

Phil464me: Ok, I love you, honey.

MAC11222: I love you, too. Bye

Phil464me: bye

October 15, 2006

Phil464me: hi

MAC11222: whats up?

Phil464me: So, how's your arm feeling? Pretty sore?

MAC11222: not really actually

Phil464me: Good deal!

MAC11222: today i took off the bandage

MAC11222: it feels fine but it looks like some frankenstine crap

Phil464me: Hey did you get to keep the bullet?

MAC11222: yep

Phil464me: Cool! Maybe you can make a necklace or something out of it.....lol

MAC11222: yea thats what i plan on doing :)

MAC11222: Can you pray for my friend bishop?

MAC11222: he was the other guy that got hit

17

Phil464me: How's he doing?

MAC11222: he's going to live

Phil464me: So, what was the extent of his injuries?

MAC11222: but they took the bottom part of his lung, one of his kidneys, and his spleen

Phil464me: Oh my gosh!!! Was that from shrapnel?

Phil464me: Or did he have bullets, too?

MAC11222: that was one bullet

Phil464me: Lord, in the name of Jesus, we lift Bishop up to you. You are the father of miracles, God. You are the supreme physician. Thank you, God, that you are healing Bishop TOTALLY, COMPLETELY, and that he will be whole again, amen.

Phil464me: Oh my gosh, John! I did not realize he was injured that badly. YOU really WERE fortunate not to have been injured any worse than you were!!

MAC11222: yea i know

MAC11222: and he was in a high back

MAC11222: which is much more protected then i was

Phil464me: So, you'll agree that God was protecting you!

Phil464me: AND continues to protect you, in Jesus' name, amen!!

MAC11222: yep

Phil464me: So, where is Bishop now?

MAC11222: he should be in Germany i think

MAC11222: well gotta go. I love you

Phil464me: I love you, too, John. bye

What a miracle that was! God was true to His word: "If you ask anything in my name, it will be done for you." We had asked that God protect John every minute of every day, which is exactly what He did. Yes, John was shot, but he wasn't hurt!

On October 17th, I received a call at my office from John. "Hi, Mom!"

"Hi, John! How's it goin'?"

"Good, how's it goin' with you?"

"Good!" Then, suddenly realizing the wonder of this call, "Is this a social call or did you get injured again?"

He broke the news, "I got injured again."

"John! This is serious...don't mess with me..." He was always making jokes. "Did you REALLY get injured again?"

"Yep," he answered matter-of-factly, "I got shot again."

"You sound so good...where are you?"

"I'm at the hospital."

"Oh my gosh!" My heart leapt into my throat. "Are you all right?"

"Yep, I'm fine."

"So, what happened?"

"Well," he began, "I was in the turret again, and we came under attack...again, and this time the bullet went in the front of my right arm and out the back."

Panic rifled through me. "Oh my gosh! Tell me about your arm! Are you SURE you're all right?"

"Yep, they've got me bandaged up, but I'm okay." Then, trying to divert my focus, he announced, "Hey, I'm going to be in the *Stars & Stripes* newspaper."

Successfully diverted, I responded, "Oh, John! That's great! That's wonderful!" Even though I'd never heard of it I told him... "I can't wait to read it!" I'm thinking *Stars and Stripes* would list *Those injured this week were...*

19

October 18, 2007

Phil464me: hey

MAC11222: wassup

MAC11222: so how is everything going?

Phil464me: Good!

Phil464me: So R U like bored out of your gord?

MAC11222: for the most part

MAC11222: its cool because no one gives me any crap either

JOHN ON HIS WAY TO THE HOSPITAL AFTER GUNSHOT WOUND #2. P.S. HE HAS SINCE GIVEN UP CIGARETTES.

MAC11222: about not doing crap

Phil464me: So, R your old buds with you there waiting on you? Lol

MAC11222: nope actually they are touring afghan

Phil464me: Touring Afghan? Like with camera's around their necks with their visers on "touring"? LOL

Phil464me: How is your arm? ? ? ?

MAC11222: i have it in a sling

MAC11222: so that i wont move it as much

Phil464me: Wound still bleeding though, right?

MAC11222: yep

Phil464me: Hard to imagine something going clean, clear through my body.....

Phil464me: Did you find the bullet? You could have a matched pair if you put it with the other one.

Phil464me: Maybe, you could make some nice cuff links or something? j/k

MAC11222: no this one went straight through

Phil464me: So, it ended up on the ground somewhere?

Phil464me: That's Ok; you don't have any cuff-linked shirts anyway.

MAC11222: gtg

MAC11222: ill talk to you later

MAC11222: bye, love you

Phil464me: I love you, too!!

MAC11222 signed off at 1:14 PM

The following week, a friend of mine from Florida e-mailed me a copy of the *Stars and Stripes* publication. On the front cover was a huge 5" X 10" picture of John with the headline, "Marine Shot Twice, Same Week, Same Arm, Answers to...Lucky." The article described what had happened and perfectly captured John's personality.

Note: The link to the *Stars and Stripes* article can be found at http://www.stripes.com/article.asp?section=104&article=31702&archive=true

Apparently, the reporter for *Stars and Stripes* had been back on base and asked some of John's friends if they knew of a good story. "Yeah!" they responded. "You need to go to the hospital and talk to McClellan! He just got shot again; that makes two times in one week!"

This was a perfect example of the scripture, *"All things work for good for those who love God and are called according to his purpose."* For the longest time, many people prayed that God and His angels would protect John and watch over him at all times. The bullet had miraculously passed through his right arm. If he had been facing one-half inch in either direction, he could have been killed, or at best, had a severely injured arm. God protected and spared him. Yes, John had been shot...twice...but he wasn't hurt!

The story about the *Stars and Stripes* article hit our local newspaper so many people in our community read about him. Further, the reporter in the Columbia Daily Tribune who wrote the article allowed me to give God the glory. Everyone knew that we had prayed and prayed for him and how it was "SO God" that John sustained two gunshot wounds, but his injuries were not serious. The people of Columbia responded to the local newspaper article with appropriate amazement of the miracles God had performed in these incidents. All things truly did work for good as John's story served as a witness to our entire community of God's miraculous power.

In January of 2007, John and his unit returned to Kaneohe Bay, Hawaii.

22

5

August, 2006

After returning from Afghanistan, John spent seven months in Hawaii and California preparing for his deployment to Iraq. On August 13, 2006, John came home for a twenty-four day leave. We were thrilled that his leave miraculously coincided with his half-sister, Jane's wedding on September 3rd.

23

One day he walked in the front door and announced, "Hey Mom! I got another tattoo today!"

"JOHN! You promised me you wouldn't get any more tattoos!" He already had two doozies!

"Didn't."

"Did."

"Didn't."

"Did!" Then, I relented, "Oh all right...whatever...let's see it."

Just below his naval about seven inches long and one and a half inch tall, was spelled L U C K Y, all in green, with a shamrock on each side, and a horseshoe for the "U."

"Well," I said, "I have to admit, of the three tattoos you've got, I do like this one the best, but please promise me, you won't get any more." Sadly, for me, he would not commit to that promise.

We had a wonderful time with him home, and the wedding was fabulous. Every one of John's relatives attended. It was an incredible gathering of family and friends, not only for the wedding, but also for John's send off, as we all knew in just a few weeks, he would be in Iraq.

On September 4th, the day after Jane's wedding, we drove John to the St. Louis airport to board the flight back to Hawaii. This departure was heart-wrenching, much more than when he left for Afghanistan. At this time, we knew John's duty station to be Haditha, Iraq, purported to be one of the most dangerous assignments in Iraq. This contributed greatly to our fears. While in Afghanistan, John and his fellow Marines earned the reputation as "bad asses" (John's words).

As a result, they were awarded the assignment to the hot spot of Haditha.

On Sunday, September 10th, we received a call from John informing us they were shipping out the next day. I thought it to be very poignant, that they would be leaving on September 11th. John relayed that he would let us know when they landed in Iraq. He warned that

24

once they settled in, the availability of computers would be limited, so we should not expect to hear from him as frequently as when he was in Afghanistan.

On the 14th, John called from Iraq. They had arrived safely.

JOHN WITH HIS SISTER, JANE, ON THE DAY OF HER WEDDING,
SEPTEMBER 3, 2006

6

September 27, 2006

The emotional comfort of knowing John had arrived safely in Haditha, contrasted vastly with our despondence after the devastating phone call we received two weeks later.

Somehow Carl and I made it through that night. By God's grace, eventually we were able to drift to sleep. I awoke around 6:30 that morning. Almost immediately, I called my sister, Marilyn, in Florida. I had hoped to reach her before she received the e-mail, but it was obvious from her voice I had not been successful in that effort.

"Oh Connie," She cried, "I am so sorry."

Together we cried. I told her, "I am so grateful that everyone in our family was able to be with John at Jane's wedding. Marilyn, if John's fate is to be a vegetable, I want God to take him."

She agreed, "You're right; it's important that you tell that to the doctors."

"I will."

I then called my other three sisters, across the country, to relay the devastating news. My oldest sister, Susan, in Quincy, Illinois volunteered to break the news to my mother, who also lives in Quincy.

My church, Family Worship Center, held early morning prayer service from 7:00 to 8:00 a.m. every weekday. The only time I'd ever attended occurred four years prior when a good friend of ours lost his arm in an auto accident. It's just not something I routinely attended, but on the morning of September 27th, I was there at 7:01! My Pastor, Tom Leuther, was standing in the back of the sanctuary next to the window where he saw and heard my truck screech to a halt in front of the church. He met me in the foyer and could see, immediately, from the look on my face that we had a serious problem. I relayed what had happened, after which we stood and prayed.

27

In retrospect, I realized our prayer in the foyer that morning was when I crossed the threshold from fear into faith. Up to that moment I had been paralyzed with fear and not optimistic about John's condition.

Pastor Tom and I proceeded into the sanctuary where I was immediately surrounded by the morning worshippers, who continued to pray with me.

I proclaimed, "I've done everything God has told me to do to keep this from happening. I prayed for John everyday, I prayed Psalm 91 over him every day, and I led my e-mail entourage in prayer for him almost every day. But…I know that all things work for good, and the only possible good to come from this is that God is going to heal him, and it's going to be the miracle of miracles and testimony of testimonies to the community!" This was my time to show God how much I trusted Him. I had to put my hope in God.

I could have said, "I've done everything God has told me to do for this not to happen. Why did He allow this to happen?" I didn't do that. Instead, I stood on God's promises of *"All things work for good for those who love God and are called according to His purpose…All things are possible with God…You cannot walk by what you hear or see, you must walk by faith…I call those things that are not as though they are."*

After calling and asking what they could do for us, my sister-in-law and brother-in-law, Lois and J.H., rushed to the house to help. They arrived just as I returned home from the prayer service. Everyone was so wonderful. Not just those who called and stopped by or brought food, but also all those praying for us. We could feel the love. In my opinion, people praying for us opened the door for God to give us everything we needed: strength, courage, rest, peace, joy and encouragement.

We had so many e-mails coming in. I wanted very much to print and save every one of them, so I asked my brother-in-law if he would mind printing and deleting them. He said he'd be happy to. After he'd been working at it for a while, I asked how it was going. Frustrated, he replied, "A minute ago I was down to 80, but now I'm back up to 135!

I laughingly responded, "Ok, well, I guess this isn't going to work. Thanks for trying."

That afternoon some friends took my e-mail list and notified everyone that they were going to hold a candlelight vigil on our front lawn at 7:30 that evening. The 6:00 evening news also relayed that notification. People met at Oakland Park, just a half block from our home, to unite in prayer. Everyone either brought or was provided a candle. My Pastors, Tom and Vicki Leuther, led a moving, prayerful appeal to God for the miraculous healing that could only come from Him at this time in John's young life. The police blocked the street from both directions so everyone could safely cross. At 7:30, I walked onto my driveway awaiting their arrival. At approximately 8:00, I looked up the street toward the park, and saw a sight I will never forget. The police parked perpendicular to the street and had their lights flashing allowing a twenty foot swath for people to cross. As dusk fell, all I could see was a flow of flickering candles as they came down the sidewalk for half a block, single file. Literally, the saints were marching in. My only regret was that I didn't have my camera.

When everyone arrived in front of our home, once again my Pastors led the assembled in prayer. A supernatural energy penetrated the air that night. Before the vigil ended, I *felt* God's assurance that He was going to heal John. In fact, I was so assured, I proclaimed it right there on our driveway. "I know John's going to be okay. I know God's going to heal him. How can God not heal him with all of you here praying? I know God is going to heal him!"

I knew what they were thinking, "Poor woman...in denial...eternal optimist..."

From there I asked that no one leave until I could give each person a hug. So, I gave each person a hug with the assurance that, "Really...really, he's going to be okay!"

Then, while I was making the rounds giving everyone a hug, an official looking military vehicle pulled up in front of our house. Out of the vehicle stepped a Marine in full dress uniform. Before me was the envisioned image that every military parent fears. My face froze as my heart pounded. *Please don't tell me what I don't want to hear.*

Almost immediately, he smiled and waved. At that point, I recognized him as the Gunny Sgt. from the local Marine Recruiting Office, who, as it turned out, had come to give his support.

For about five seconds, I had a huge faith "hiccup," quickly replaced by an even greater sigh of relief and rejuvenated faith.

Before everyone left, I announced we expected to hear from the doctor at approximately 12:15 the next morning, and I would immediately put the word out on

30

the "wire," so everyone could know the latest.

Later some of my friends told me they left in amazement, marveling at how they had come to give me comfort but ended up being comforted by me. They also told me that they, too, felt the supernatural energy of the Holy Spirit on our lawn that night.

Later that night, almost twenty-four hours to the minute after the first contact, Dr. Hill called as promised. He apologized that the neurosurgeon was not available to speak with us, but he relayed, "I don't know if I misread this report yesterday or what, but... I've got some incredible news for you."

31

7

September 28, 2006

Iknew there were dozens of people anxiously awaiting Dr. Hill's report, so immediately after hanging up from his call, I rushed to my computer to let everyone know.

From: Connie McClellan
Date: September 28, 2006 12:28 AM
Subject: Update on John

THANK YOU JESUS!!! John is doing SOOOOOO GOOD!!!
We received a call from the same doctor, Dr. Hill, with whom we spoke last night. The neurosurgeon was not available, but Dr. Hill obtained the needed information.

1.) John is doing GREAT!!
2.) He has movement in all four extremities
3.) He is responding to sensory stimuli
4.) The doctor was pretty sure that his pupils are reactive.
5.) His vital signs are good
6.) The cerebellum was not affected!! Hallaluia!!!

7.) His intracranial pressure is 12. Normal is 10-15, so that is EXCELLENT. The brain swelling is being kept to a minimum

8.) He has a very good chance of making a full recovery!!!!!!

With any luck he should be off the ventilator in the next week, at which time they can back off the sedation, so that they can tell if his eyesight is affected. The part of the brain that may have been damaged may affect his eyesight. So, this is our biggest area of concern

Please pray with me: Thank you, Lord, that John's eyesight will not be affected by this injury and, that there is nothing else that will be affected long term.

We are SOOOOOOOOO THRILLED with this report and give you all the glory, God. Thank you, thank you, thank you that you are the supreme physician, and that you have answered our prayers, in Jesus' name, amen.

33

The candlelight prayer vigil at our home last night was nothing short of FABULOUS! Thank you so much to the 100+ candle holding people who were there to pray together for God's healing of our precious John. For those of you who weren't there, it was a sight to behold. I'll never forget it as long as I live. And, I'm going to contact the local news stations to get a copy of the videos to show John with his 20/20 visioned eyes how much the people in our community love him and care about him. Carl & I were so moved by the love we felt on our front lawn.

To give you a little more information on what actually occurred, the doctor indicated that snipers are running amuck in the Haditha area and our boys are being shot right and left from afar. John was standing post when he was struck. He was wearing his helmet. The bullet went in just over his left ear, so his beautiful face will not be marred or scarred, thank you, Jesus. The bullet exited at the back of his neck on the left side.

This is nothing short of the miracle that we have been praying for. At this time, please continue to pray that his vision is not affected and that he will be sent home to Walter Reed in miraculously short time.

34

Thank you so much for your prayers. I will update you after we talk to the doctors in Germany. John left for Germany approximately 4 hours ago. We're told that it is a 5 hour flight and that we can call about 10:00 AM our time to see what his status is and to get an idea of when he'll be coming home. It is our understanding he will be sent to Walter Reed Hospital in Bethesda, MD.

I will let everyone know as soon as I get the update from Germany.

I love you ALLLLLLLLL!!! Thank you SOOOOOO much!!
Connie

Throughout the previous day, my mother and I spoke frequently, in an effort to comfort each other. On this morning, I called to give her the good news. "Oh Mom!

I've got some really good news for you!" I proceeded to pass on the report that the doctor had given us. "The concern, though, is the area of the brain that was affected could leave him permanently blind."

As long as I live, I will never forget her response, "We can do blind," she stated simply.

"You're right. We can do blind. He's young; he can learn Braille. We can all learn Braille. We can do a family Braille thing or whatever." Normally, being blind would be such a devastating prognosis, but no...we can do blind.

Needless to say, my mother was thrilled with Dr. Hill's report. All of the sudden, our priorities were *so* in order. How grateful we were for this report, that he was alive and doing as well as we could have hoped.

35

At the end of our second discussion with Dr. Hill at midnight on September 27th, he provided the telephone number for the hospital in Germany. He then advised us that John should be in Germany by 10:00 AM our time on Thursday, September 28th.

The week preceding John's injury, our long distance carrier went out of business. As a result I changed to Mediacom, which suited our needs perfectly except that the new plan, as described by the sales representative, would not accommodate international calls. I didn't give this any consideration as we've never needed international service anyway. Little did I know, a week later, we would desperately need that service to call the hospital in Germany.

With John in transit, we frantically attempted to contact the hospital in Landstuhl using our cell phone. Sadly our cell phone would not allow international calls either. On a whim, we tried to call from the Mediacom land line. It went through without a hitch! This, to me, was the first of many, "I will not leave you or forsake you" touches we received from God throughout our time following John's injury.

From: Connie McClellan
Date: September 28, 2006 11:30 AM
Talked to the Doctor in Germany re: John

We just got off the phone with the doctor in Germany. Here's what we've got:

1.) John's doing very well ESPECIALLY considering what he's been through.

2.) He responds to commands such as lift your right hand, lift your left leg, etc. so he can hear and comprehend

3.) He needs to stay on a ventilator a few more days to be sure his airway will remain open. Many times with brain injuries this can be a problem; however, he has shown some signs of breathing on his own.

4.) They are flying him to Bethesda National Naval Center in MD TOMORROW, which is AWESOME!!

5.) His vitals are still good.

6.) They have reduced the sedation which is good.

7.) The shock waves from an AK47 in the brain can cause problems, so we'll have to wait and see on that, as well as the amount of brain tissue that they had to remove. The areas of concern are vision and speech.

Please do not back off of your prayers for his complete recovery until we have the confirmation from his doctors.

Thank you so much!

Love to all,
Connie

(CORRECTION) At the time of this e-mail, we thought the bullet was from an AK-47, but we later learned, it was a 5.56 mm round.

That afternoon, we were contacted by the Marine Liaison's office at the National Naval Medical Center in Bethesda, Maryland. Initially, we thought we would be flying to Germany; however, John's recuperation had miraculously progressed to the point he would be immediately flown to Bethesda. John had endured the critical surgery in Balad on the 26th, was flown to Germany for evaluation on the 28th, and arrived on home soil on the 29th...amazing!!

Here were the miracles we had received up to this point:

1.) The first bullet wound sustained in Afghanistan did not cause permanent damage

2.) The second bullet wound in Afghanistan did not cause permanent damage.

3.) John sustained a gunshot to the head and lived.

4.) Within 24 hours John's prognosis went from "if he survives, he will more than likely being a vegetable" to "He's responding positively to every test and could make a full recovery."

5.) Shot in the head on Tuesday, he was able to be air transported to the United States on Friday.

8

September 29 -30, 2006

From: Connie McClellan
Date: September 29, 2006 10:00 AM
Subject: Update

I am THRILLED to relay that John will be in Bethesda TODAY! In fact, he should be arriving anytime. Shot in the head In Iraq on Tuesday, and in the US on Friday! UNBELIEVABLE! NO...MIRACLE!!

39

Carl, Jane, & I are leaving tomorrow, Carl & I from St. Louis, Jane from Chicago. We will rendezvous in Washington and the Marines will pick us up from the airport, deliver us to our hotel, and arrange for everything. WOW... I am so impressed with how they have helped us. They called yesterday to tell me they're expecting John to arrive on Friday, and when would we like for them to book our flight. We all know what a pain it is making flight & hotel arrangements, so this is such a blessing, not to mention that they're providing for everything. Wow....

I'm taking my laptop, so I will keep everyone informed on John's progress.

We are specifically praying for vision, speech and, of course, full mental function. He is still sedated, so he hasn't opened his eyes, and he is still on a ventilator, so couldn't talk if he wanted to. We are believing for a 100% recovery, so don't stop praying until we get that confirmation.

Words cannot express what it has meant to Carl & myself, the outpouring of love and prayers that we have received in the past 48 hours. Thank you all so much.

Love, Connie

On Friday, September 29th, I received a call from the Columbia office of U.S. Representative, Kenny Hulshof. The gentlemen who called told me Representative Hulshof tried to get into the NNMC hospital to see John, but because he wasn't family, he was not allowed in. At that point, I joked, "Kenny should have told them he was my brother!" We laughed.

On Saturday, Carl and I sat in the Columbia Regional Airport anxiously awaiting our departure to Bethesda. Ironically, only moments later, we saw Representative Hulshof, who had just deplaned from D.C. We introduced ourselves and I thanked him for attempting to visit John and I shared the 'pretending to be my brother' joke. We laughed.

While on the plane, I thought about a little stuffed Panda Bear, "Pandy," that Carl had given John when John had minor surgery at the age of four . When John was six years old, Jane underwent surgery after which John generously presented her with Pandy. How I wish I'd thought to ask Jane to bring Pandy to Bethesda...that is...if she still had it. Oh well...

When we rendezvoused with Jane in Bethesda, I told her, "Oh Jane, I meant to call you before you left, to see if you still have the Panda Bear that John gave you."

"You mean this Panda Bear?" She pulled Pandy out of her bag, and continued, "It was so weird; I thought of Pandy and went down to my storage room to see if I could find him. I expected to have to go through a ton of boxes, but there he was sitting right on top as if he was waiting for me to come and get him. It was very cool."

This was just...*so*...God!

41

This incident exemplified one of the many little coincidental miracles that God did for us, touching us and giving us His assurance that, "I'm still here; I will not leave you or forsake you."

Jane, Carl and I met with the Marine Liaison representative on the main floor of the hospital.

We spent forty-five grueling minutes going through the necessary paperwork for our stay. Every minute that passed made me more anxious to get upstairs to see John.

Okay, where do we sign, what more do we need to do? Can we get on with it?

Finally, we were escorted to the ICU waiting room where a nurse waited to take us to see John. As we made our way down the endless hallway, we wanted so badly to see him, but at the same time, we were terrified of what we might see. I had prepared myself to see John with his head the size of a basketball, wrapped in bandages, like in an old WWII movie. It wasn't that way at all; he looked amazing! He had no bandages; however, he lay in the midst of a shocking maze of tubes protruding from his body and crisscrossing in every direction. He had a breathing tube, a brain shunt, nose feeding tube, and other intravenous, medication tubes. They warned us that he would not be awake, but they were gradually reducing his medication, so that by morning, he should emerge from his medically induced coma.

42

From: Connie McClellan
Date: September 30, 2006
Subject: Update on John from Connie, Carl & Jane in Bethesda

Ok everyone!! We arrived about 5:00 and went to the hospital immediately after checking into our hotel. I'll give you more details on that tomorrow, but for now I'm going to cut to the chase.

We were able to see John, but he was not conscious, because earlier today they tried to extubate (take out the breathing tube) him; however, his vocal chords were too swollen, so they had to intubate him again, which meant they had to heavily sedate him again. Consequently, he did not respond to our being there, which, of course was disappointing. BUT, tomorrow we are hopeful with the sedation reduced that he will have his eyes open.

Today before we were there, he had his eyes open and was following the nurse as she was talking and moving around him. They are optimistic about his vision. They did the testing on his brain to see if the blood was flowing appropriately and ....IT IS.. Praise the Lord! At the moment he has some air around his lungs, so they have done another x-ray to see if they might have to put a tube in his lung. If they do, it is just temporary, and is not a serious concern. His face is not affected, Praise God. He is still as beautiful as ever. His left ear drum was perforated, so we won't know until he's conscious, whether that will be a permanent problem. We know he can hear, though, because he hears their commands. Specifically, Balance, Vision, speech, left ear hearing and full mental functions are the areas that we won't know are ok until he is fully conscious, so KEEP ON PRAYING!!

43

We have to wear gowns, gloves and masks, because when the Marines and soldiers come back from Iraq, they have Iraq bacteria that can be epidemic in the hospital because of the all of the open wounds. This was very frustrating because we couldn't kiss him. When we are in the room, we have to wear the garb, and then we disrobe outside his room and the gowns, etc are discarded.

There was another mom who was in the waiting room whose son, Will, was injured by an IED that imbedded a rock through his left eye through to the back of his head. Also, both of his hands are badly injured. Please pray for his recovery, and for his family.

Love to All!
Connie

We left the hospital and settled into the Navy Lodge which provided very comfortable rooms with two queen beds, a kitchenette with burners, a microwave, and a small refrigerator. Little did we know this room would be our home for the next 3 ½ weeks. Our hotel was six blocks from the hospital which afforded us the perfect exercise opportunity each day as we walked to the NNMC. We were fortunate the weather was beautiful – warm and sunny for the majority of our stay. We slept well that first night and really, all of the subsequent nights as God blessed us with restful sleep to sustain us during that critical time. I attributed all of God's blessings to His responding to the prayers of the hundreds of people who were praying for us.

The next morning we arrived about 8:00 and made our way back to John in the ICU. As we stood outside of his room, putting on our protective garb, we could see that he was awake. He told me later that he saw Carl, Jane, and me, and he knew we were familiar, but wasn't exactly sure who we were. He was pretty sure we were related, but it took him a while to figure it out. I didn't take offense as he also told me he didn't know who he was either. Fortunately, he didn't "wig" out about it. Of course, he was so heavily sedated, he probably couldn't have "wigged" out if he wanted to.

As we prepared to see him, the staff told us, "Be sure to remind John where he is and what has happened." They explained that being in Iraq was the last thing he remembered. Then *poof*, he's in a hospital and we're there. So naturally, his first thought was, "What are they doing in Iraq?" We proceeded to tell John, "You were on patrol in Iraq, and you were shot in the head by a sniper. You're doing great. You're at the Bethesda National Naval Medical Center in the United States."

One of the common problems with a traumatic brain injury is the short-term memory loss can be severe, especially early on. For that reason, it was important that we kept repeating what happened, where he was, and what was happening now.

45

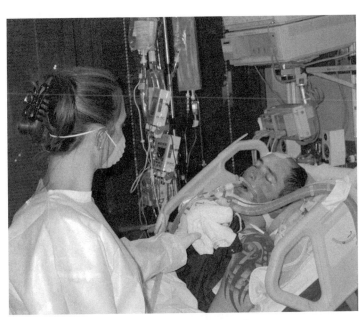

JOHN IN ICU WITH SISTER, JANE.

9

October 1, 2006 – October 3, 2006

From: Connie McClellan
Subject: Update from Bethesda RE: John
Date: Sun, 1 Oct 2006 10:17:03 -0500

46

We've got a WONDERFUL REPORT!

Today we were able to see John and he was awake! I asked if he could see me - to squeeze my hand, and.... HE DID!! He still has the ventilator in and it's very obvious that he HATES it, but we've explained to him until the vocal chords swelling goes down that he has to have the ventilator in because breathing is REALLY IMPORTANT!!

We told him how everyone has been so concerned and they're all praying for him. We joked with him about something (can't remember exactly what it was), but you could tell he was trying to laugh. I was holding his hand, when Dad kiddingly told him that his hard-headedness has finally started to work to his advantage. Then, Carl & I started bantering about whether he got his hard head from

Carl or me. At that time, I was holding his hand and said, "John if you got your hardheadedness from your Dad, squeeze my hand. He DIDN'T! I couldn't believe it! (These men always stick together). Then, he lifted his finger and curled it to motion for dad to come to him. It was too wonderful! It meant he still had his sense of humor. We laughed and laughed! What a miraculous blessing.

Then Jane got to "squeeze-talk" with him for a few minutes, but it was obvious he was getting very tired, so we "squeeze asked" if he wanted to rest and he said yes, so now we're in the waiting room, making the anticipated calls and this e-mail.

We spoke with the doctor; she said he's doing really well, but they are concerned about the vocal chords. There does not seem to be much activity, but it's too early to say, so please continue to pray:

47

Lord, we thank you that you are restoring John to 100%, and that he will be able to talk, see, walk, run, and do anything else that he ever wants to do (except to go back to Iraq, but that is certainly his call). Lord, you have done the miracle of miracles so far with this situation, and we believe that you are taking him to 100%. We love you and appreciate you so much for the peace, love and confidence you have given us throughout this ordeal, in Jesus' precious name. Amen.

Love, Connie

Since John's left hand was extremely weak, he didn't use it at all. So when he squeeze-talked, he used his right hand.

During the seven days John was in the ICU the nurses told us not to expect him to remember much, as he was continually given an intravenous painkiller which the nurses jokingly labeled "milk of amnesia." It was true. John was so "in and out" that he didn't remember much of what had gone on during that week. He tired easily, so he slept more often than not.

During that ICU time, John had only been vertical once which was to take a "swallow test" that he failed miserably. Consequently, he had to receive his nourishment through a tube inserted through his nose. This tube was so annoying that, without realizing what he was doing, John would pull the nose tube out during the night. Then, the next morning the doctors would have to reinsert, which was not a fun thing for John. Finally, the doctors surgically inserted a feeding tube into his stomach, making him much more comfortable.

Immediately after John's original surgery in Balad, he had a shunt inserted in the top of his head to relieve the pressure on the brain. There were two prerequisites for John to be able to leave the ICU:

1.) His blood pressure had to stabilize, and
2.) The brain shunt had to be gone, which meant the swelling also had to stabilize.

We anxiously awaited these physiological improvements, as it also meant that John was "out of the woods." Every day after walking to the hospital, Jane, Carl, and I took turns visiting John. With brain trauma injuries, patients must not be over-stimulated, so we limited John's visits to one person at a time. Since he slept most of the time, when it was my turn to be with him, rather than talking, I sang to him. More specifically, I sang the Lord's Prayer...over and over. Just singing that prayer gave me a tremendous peace, at a time when peace was not warranted. This was where the "milk of amnesia" worked well for John, as he doesn't remember my terrible singing voice at all.

For John to talk took a tremendous amount of his energy. Consequently, he would use the "thumbs up" or "thumbs down" signs in lieu of talking. In addition, in the past, John had never been one to go to bed early, or to take naps, but my, oh my...just the least little thing would wear him out. Most of his time in the ICU was spent sleeping.

Since the number of visitors he could have was limited, we spent much of our time in the waiting room. If anyone new arrived, I always introduced myself and asked who they were there for. Most were family and friends of soldiers or Marines injured in Iraq, but some were there for civilian patients as well. One gentleman was there for his sister who had an aneurysm and was in a coma. I asked if I could pray with him for his sister. He seemed grateful for the offer, so we prayed together. Later when Carl came in and I introduced him to this gentleman, we began talking about John. The man had assumed I was a church volunteer and was shocked when he learned I was there for my son. He said he couldn't believe how cheerful and calm I was considering my son had just been shot in the head. This was another example of God's grace giving me the peace and fortitude that can only come from Him at a time such as this.

Within two days of our arrival, the hospital chaplain, Willie Williams, visited and prayed with us, giving us much needed encouragement. He relayed that the Bethesda NNMC ICU witnesses a constant flow of miracles. Willie spoke of the many military men and women who had come to NNMC with the most extreme injuries, yet they recovered. In his opinion, God's miracle working power was responsible for their amazing recoveries, as their injuries were too extreme for medical science to receive the credit. Willie expounded, "With most successful medical recoveries, it's easy to give the doctors credit, the therapy credit, or the medication credit for the success. But in these situations, there is only one explanation and that is that God has intervened in a miraculous way."

The day after we met Willie, he returned to give us an incredible, full-sized quilt with the label 'Quilt of Valor' embroidered on it. Quilts of Valor are quilted by women all over the country and presented to the wounded Marines and soldiers. Willie expressed he wanted me to have it because he knew I would send a thank you note. Instantly I replied, "The thank you note will be in the mail today!" That afternoon I mailed a thank you note to Carolyn Townsend, the woman who made John's quilt. Almost immediately I received an e-mail from her and then added her to my e-mail list.

In the waiting room, we met the family of a young Army helicopter mechanic named Daniel, who flew from Germany on the same plane as John. Daniel was injured by a mortar attack that threw shrapnel from the left side of his head straight through to the right. Daniel had not regained consciousness during the three weeks we were at NNMC.

A third soldier on that same plane, Will, suffered an IED explosion injury when a half-dollar sized rock was blown through his left eye into the back of his brain. It was uncertain if the doctors were going to attempt to remove the rock as it would probably cause him additional problems. Will became John's roommate after we moved out of the ICU to the 5th floor.

51

From: Connie McClellan
Subject: Update on John's doctor's report
Date: Mon, 2 Oct 2006 16:37:23 -0500

We just spoke with the doctors. They're going to try for the second time to remove John's breathing tube. This is so important, not only because he HATES it, but also because that's why he is sedated. So, once that thing is out, we'll know much better where he is in relation to where he's GOING to be.

We did learn that the bullet may have severed the nerve that controls the left side of his face. Consequently, he can't quite close his left eye and his smile is one-sided, but DO NOT DESPAIR.

They have a procedure where they take nerves from his ankle and insert in his face. I know this works because the young Marine who drove us from the airport was injured in Iraq and they did the same thing for his hand. They took the nerve out of his ankle and put in his hand, and it's working really well. So, this is not just some far-fetched, experimental procedure. This is something they do all the time.

Anyway, please pray with me: Thank you, Lord, that the tube will come out and John's airway will be clear so that he doesn't have to have the tracheotomy. Also, thank you, Lord, that the nerve transplant from the ankle will take place soon and be successful. And, we continue to thank you for full mental function, balance, speech and vision. Also, Lord, we continue to thank you for the healing that you are doing in Daniel & Will. Also, thank you, Lord, that you continue to protect John's buds in Hadita, in Jesus' name. Amen

Thank you so much for your prayers. Keep 'em comin'!

Love, Connie

From: Connie McClellan
Subject: Update on John, Pastor Tom coming for lunch
Date: Tue, 3 Oct 2006 08:31:02 -0500

It's going to be a BIG DAY here at Bethesda National Naval Center!! John gets his breathing tube out and he is SOOOOOOOO looking forward to it. Please pray that all systems are go for the tube to come out and stay out and that he not have to have a tracheotomy.

I just got a call from my church. My pastor, Tom Leuther from Family Worship Center, is going to be here for lunch!! Oh my gosh.......I am so touched and thrilled!

Please pass this along to anyone that you know: Thank you so much for the prayer support that you have given to John and our family. We can feel the love, and it has truly helped us get through this ordeal.

Anyway, I can't wait for my next e-mail to you.

Love, Connie

I'll never forget Jane coming into the waiting room to tell me the doctors were preparing to remove the breathing tube. My eyes welled with tears as I replied, "Oh, Jane, I don't think I can watch. Can you be with him, and then let me know as soon as it's over?"

53

Up to this time, I'd been a pretty brave mom. However, the thought of watching the doctors remove the breathing tube with the possibility of having to put it back in, was more than I could handle at this particular moment.

"No problem. You stay here. Dad and I will be there with him. I'll let you know as soon as we know the outcome." Praise God Jane and Carl were willing and able to be in there, so that I didn't have to.

However, the good to come from my being in the waiting room during the tube removal process was that it allowed me to send out the urgent prayer request from the waiting room computer.

From: Connie McClellan
Re: Ok...this is it. They're taking the breathing tube out right now. Please pray.
10/3/06 9:57 AM

Jane just came in to the waiting room to tell me they're doing it!! They're taking the tube out in just a few minutes. I don't want to be there, but Jane & Carl are going to be, so Jane will come back and tell me when it's over.

Thank you, Lord that this extubation will go PERFECTLY in Jesus' name.

Love, Connie

From: Connie McClellan
Subject: It is DONE!!! THE BREATHING TUBE WAS REMOVED SUCCESSFULLY!!
Date: Tue, 3 Oct 2006 10:28:15 -0500

54

It is out!!! And he is breathing on his own. That's all for now!! Thank you EVERYBODY for your prayers! Right now one vocal chord is visibly active, the other is not moving yet, so please pray about that.

Love to all,
Connie

Now that he had the breathing tube out, we were able to learn the answers to a myriad of questions: 1.) Can he swallow? 2.) How well can he see? 3.) How well can he hear? 4.) How is he...cognitively? 4.) Can he talk? 5.) Can he remember?

The first deficiency realized after removing the breathing tube was that John could not swallow. This presented a *huge* concern. Our question to the doctors was, "Is his inability to swallow caused by the brain or was it because of the swelling created by the breathing tube?" The doctors could not yet answer this question; only time would tell.

Another problem noticed immediately after the breathing tube removal, John only had the use of one vocal chord. Again we asked that ever present question, "Is this caused by the breathing tube, or the brain?" Again, the doctors could not answer unequivocally.

Consequently, we immediately began praying for God to restore the non-responsive vocal chord. In the meantime, we chided him by calling him "Marlon Brando, Junior." Of course, he had no idea who Marlon Brando was, so we gave him the verbal "Cliff's notes" on *The Godfather.*

During his stay at the NNMC, we experienced many miracles in many forms which can only be attributed to God's grace and answers to the prayers of the hundreds, thousands, and maybe even millions of people praying for him. I truly believe the prayers of the people allowed us strength, courage, rest, peace and even joy; we felt the love.

I also believe the prayers of the people moved God to continually orchestrate little coincidental happenstances that I came to call Godsidences. I don't believe coincidences are coincidental; I always view them as a sign from God. All of these "coincidences" were just little "touches" from God that continually ministered, "I'm still here...I will not leave you or forsake you."

An example of a "Godsidence" began on the morning of October 2nd when we received a with a call from the financial manager of my church. "I just wanted to give you a heads up. Pastor Tom is on a plane to have lunch with you today."

My mouth dropped open, "He's going to have lunch with me... *Here*?"

He continued, "Yes, he's on his way."

56

After he arrived, Pastor Tom told me they waited until he was on the plane before they called, as they weren't sure what my reaction would be. They considered the possibility that, for whatever reason, I might not want him to come. By waiting until he had already boarded the plane, if I responded negatively, they could say, "Too bad...he's on his way."

It didn't take Pastor Tom long to realize how happy and grateful we were to have him with us. In one day, he made quite a trek, flying from Columbia, Missouri to Bethesda AND back to Columbia. The Marine Liaisons' office said they had never known a pastor to fly in to visit a patient. Pastor Tom told us that when he announced to our congregation that he was considering making the trip, everyone stood and applauded. He interpreted that response as a confirmation of what he felt God was telling him to do.

I called Pastor Tom's visit a "Godsidence" because, of all the days for him to come to NNMC, that particular day proved to be the most critical. Unbeknownst to him or myself, that was the day the doctors were going to remove John's breathing tube. (One thing I learned throughout our NNMC "experience" was that you never knew exactly what was going to happen or when.) The removal of the breathing tube would provide a huge milestone, but was also a source of huge fear for us, because the doctors weren't positive John would be able to breathe on his own. Secondly, once they removed the breathing tube, we would find out so much more about John's condition, good or bad. This event promoted exciting, yet terrifying emotions for everyone involved. Having Pastor Tom with us helped to strengthen our faith, and confront and squelch our fears.

57

Pastor Tom treated Carl, Jane, and me individually to lunch. Whoever didn't go to lunch spent time suctioning John's saliva every few minutes. During Pastor Tom's visit, we prayed fervently about the swallowing issue. By the next morning, we only had to suction John every hour and a half, allowing us to cross another permanent disability off our list, and to add another miracle to our rapidly growing record book. *Thank you, Jesus!*

In addition, while Pastor Tom was there, he visited throughout the waiting room and ward, praying for all

the patients and families he could "lay his hands on."
Everyone appreciated his presence and prayers.

10

October 4, 2006 – October 7, 2006

From: Connie McClellan
Date: 10/4/06 7:38 AM
RE: Visit with neurosurgeon

59

I wanted to let everyone know about yesterday. I was in the middle of sending an e-mail when Carl rushed in and said the neurosurgeon was ready to talk to us. This is the first time that we had had the opportunity to talk with him.

First of all, this is one of the best neurosurgeons in the country. His name is Dr. Rocco Armonda. He has seen hundreds of these types of injuries. He was in Iraq for two years working at the hospitals there and is now here at Bethesda. Here is what he told us: "First, I must tell you, 99 out of 100 people with the type of injury that John sustained do not survive. Secondly, the bullet missed his carotid artery by a thickness of two sheets of paper. And, finally, I saw that shamrock tattoo...to say he's lucky is no joke."

I am so humbled.

Dr. Armonda did say though, that John is still not

out of the woods in the area of brain swelling. They have to watch him very closely. Consequently, he will be in ICU for at least another week. He said by the end of next week, he should be out of the woods. Needless to say, that's how we need to pray.

He said John's prognosis is good, but it will take intensive therapy. I have NO PROBLEM WITH THAT!! It's in God's hands. If He wants him to be 100% tomorrow, of course, I'm great with that, but if it takes 6 mos, a year, 2 years.......I know it is for a reason. His ways are higher than ours. I've always believed, if God doesn't answer our specific prayers immediately, it's either because A.) He's working on it or B.) He has a better plan.

60

Please pray: Lord, we thank you so much for the miracle that you have done in John's mind and body. We thank you that he will get through this critical two week period and ultimately will be 100% recovered, in Jesus' name. Amen.

In that he has had a respiratory tube in his throat for the past week, his swallowing muscles are not where they need to be. Thank you, Lord, that you are fixing that, in Jesus' name.

I'm not sure how much I'll be able to keep in touch today, as Carl, Jane and I are working fervently with him using a suction device to remove the saliva until such time as he can swallow.

Thank you to everyone for your prayers.

Love, Connie

According to Dr. Armonda, the doctors in Balad did an amazing job with John's surgery.

I have often wished I could find out more information

about who they were, as I would love to be able to "show and tell" them what an incredible job they did. It would surely be a wonderful encouragement for them.

From: Connie McClellan
Subject: Update on John McClellan
Date: Wed, 4 Oct 2006 18:40:32 -0500

Hi, everyone. I am Connie's sister, Kathy. Connie called this evening as she didn't want to monopolize the computer, and asked me to spread the good word to all of you on John's condition. He had a very good day and is breathing without the tube in his throat. He can talk, and according to Connie, he sounds a bit like Marlon Brando. They were thrilled to hear his voice, even if it was a bit hoarse. He remarked on his cute nurse, Anna (his exact words were "she kicks ass"), and this meant his eye sight is very good!! Connie sounded very upbeat, as usual. Connie, Carl, and Jane all thank you for your continued support in prayers. Thank you, Kathy
Kathy Palan, Coordinator of Continuing Education
University of Mississippi

For at least a week after the removal of John's breathing tube, swallowing continued to be a struggle. John could not use the suctioning device on his own as his arms were still too weak, so we assisted him. One day his nurse, Anna, handed me the suctioning device to use on John. John whispered in his new Marlon Brandon voice, "Thank you."

Anna responded, "He always says thank you. Tell him he doesn't have to say thank you all the time."

I exclaimed indignantly, "I'm not going to tell him that! It took me twenty years to get him to do that, and I don't want you telling him that either!" We all laughed, but at the same time, I was proud of his manners with the staff. Of course, Anna had an especially pretty face and figure, so that may have helped to promote his exemplary behavior in this particular instance.

From: Connie McClellan
Subject: Update on John
Date: Thu, 5 Oct 2006 08:41:05-0500

As I am typing this e-mail John is downstairs taking a swallow test. If he passes, he'll be able to eat and drink through his mouth....TODAY!! This is great news, as he told me before going down that he is STARVING! Please pray:

Lord, thank you that John will pass his test with flying colors and will be able to eat real food today, in Jesus' name.

Yesterday, Bird Colonel Boyle came to visit John and presented him with a special award. Sadly, I wasn't there when he presented it, but Carl and Jane were. They said John immediately "laid at attention" (same as standing at attention, only it when he's laying down) when he saw Bird Colonel Boyle walk in his room. He was presented with the pin, and John said in his new Marlon Brando voice, "Thank you, sir." Where is the camera when you need it!?!?!?!? AGHHHH!!

Anyway, what a cool story, eh? The award was not the purple heart, but it was relevant to the 3rd Marine Echo Company. Bird Colonel Boyle is the TOP, TOP, TOP of that regiment. I'm not sure how many men would be under his direction, but it's a LOT!!

Anyway, I'll let you know how the swallow test comes out. I should know within the hour.

Love, Connie

Well,........ sorry to relay John flunked his swallow test. So, at this point, they'll put a feeding tube down through his nose, which is not comfortable going down, but once it's down, he won't even know it's there. So, he'll be nice and full soon. He is swallowing his saliva very well, though, so we're very hopeful he'll pass the test on the next round. They'll try it again in a couple of days.

63

The good news is that his blood pressure meds are being stopped today. AND, it's very possible his shunt may be removed as early as Monday. (This is relieving the swelling in his brain). Those are the two conditions that are keeping him in ICU. So, prayerfully on Monday, he'll be moved from the ICU 3rd Floor to the 5th floor. Please keep that in your prayers as well as the swallowing thing.

Later.....
Connie

Sadly, John failed his swallow test which meant that he couldn't eat solid food, so a feeding tube was inserted

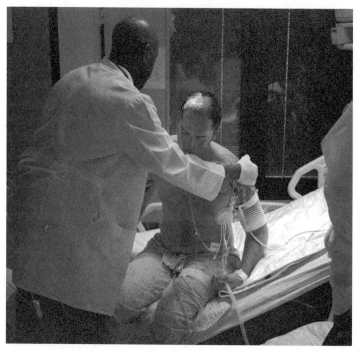

JOHN SITTING UP FOR THE FIRST TIME, ON HIS WAY TO HIS FIRST SWALLOW TEST.

through his nose. One good thing, though, was that the saliva swallowing issue had resolved itself, so we were able to cross another permanent disability off our list.

From the very first day of our arrival at NNMC, the doctors and staff strongly encouraged us to interact with other parents. The staff explained the most therapeutic thing we could do would be to open up to others about what we were going through. Sharing our emotions with others experiencing similar situations created a bond like no other.

Outside our hotel accommodations was the designated smoking area with several tables and about

20 chairs. I wasn't a smoker, but Carl was, and many of the other parents were as well.

This area not only served as the smoking section, but it had become the social area where families gathered. As a result, early on, we became well acquainted with a number of the families there.

While at the hospital, I told all the family members I met, "I know you don't smoke, but you have to come to the smoking section at the hotel .It is so therapeutic to interact with other family members." We shared, laughed, and cried, and this provided the perfect conclusion to our long and emotionally exhausting days.

From: Connie McClellan
Subject: Update at the end of today
Date: Thu, 5 Oct 2006 16:28:30-0500

The tube has been removed from John's lung....Next week, probably Wednesday, they will be inserting a piece of gold to weight his eyelid down so that his left eye will close while he sleeps. If it doesn't close, it could cause damage to his cornea. So, in the meantime, his left eye is heavily lubricated and taped shut when he's sleeping. Ultimately, they will probably do the nerve transplant procedure; however, that would be a surgery that is serious, so he's not quite ready to go through that yet. They anticipate that to be a couple of months down the road.

If he is not able to pass the swallow test, it will not be a problem ultimately, as the right side of his throat somehow will compensate for the left side, so no matter what, he will eventually be able to enjoy Carl & my cooking again.

That's pretty much all I know for now. I'm having major problems with my laptop, so I'm using the computer in the ICU waiting room, which so far, so good. Say a prayer for my laptop..lol

Love, Connie

66

Adding to my distress during John's stay in ICU, my laptop shot "craps." I called Dell, and at first they thought the problem was my power cord, so they ordered another cord. In the meantime, the Marine Liaisons had a loaner they said I could use, but they stipulated that after five days, I would need to give it back for others to use. I'm thinking, *That's perfect! By that time, I'll have my new power cord and I'll be good to go!*

Sadly, the power cord was not the problem. Dell then determined that my hard drive had blown up or something. By the sixth day, no one had come around to retrieve my hospital-issued computer, so I reluctantly made my way down to the Liaison's office, and inquired, "Uh, guys, I've had this laptop for about six days; do I need to give it back?" The Liaison representative replied, "Oh no, don't worry about it; we'll come get it if we need it."

The laptop police never came! THANK YOU, JESUS! I was able to keep it for our entire stay at NNMC, which allowed me to be with John all the time and still be able

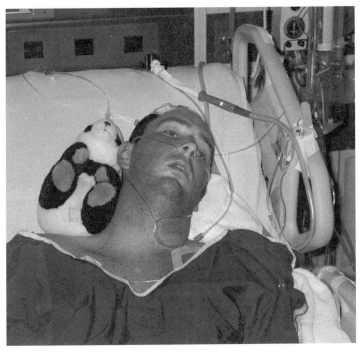

John with Pandy, immediately after the removal of the breathing tube.

to send and receive encouragement and prayers via e-mail. This, to me, was *SO* God for a couple of reasons. First, the fact that my laptop was not operational was a sign that I wasn't supposed to do my insurance work. I have a program on my laptop that allows me to access my work by computer from anywhere, but due to security concerns, the program cannot be installed on foreign computers. The second reason was the fact that I was able to keep that loaner laptop for the entire three and one-half weeks we were at NNMC and this gave me the opportunity to relay God's miracle working power to the thousands of people tuned in to this story.

Our next goal, moving out of ICU, hinged on the stabilization of John's blood pressure and the removal of the shunt in his head.

From: Connie McClellan
Subject: FW: Update at the end of today
Date: Fri, 6 Oct 2006 07:05:13-0500

Good Morning, everyone!
Ok, WELL!!!.. yesterday, as we were finishing up our visit with John, the nurse told us they are going to do a CAT scan on him this morning, and..if all is good.. they're going to take the shunt out of his head!!! This is incredible news! Just yesterday morning, they said they thought they were looking at Monday. This would put us 3 days ahead of schedule.

Please pray: Thank you, Lord, that the CAT scan results will allow the doctors to remove the shunt from John's head, in Jesus' name, Amen.

THIS means, he can be moved out of ICU. It would be a HUGE day at Bethesda National Naval Center, if that would occur!!

Also, we have another great update. Carl & Jane & I were talking about it being the month of October, and got to talking about Halloween and reflecting on when John was young. He remembers it all!! He remembers the fireman's suit that he wore when he was 5, and how he wanted to wear the skeleton suit just like the one his best friend Jon Stillwell had. WE WERE SO HAPPY to have that conversation. This means his long term memory is intact.
Then, he and Jane were joking about some movie

68

they've seen lately (something about a 40 year old virgin?) Anyway, they were reflecting on the funny lines in that movie. So, this means his short term memory is in tact, too.

This is great news. Each day we are eliminating one concern after another.

I'm preparing to go in and see him now, so I'll report as soon as I can. We've received word that three more boys are arriving today from Iraq, so the computer may be hard to access, and I certainly don't want to monopolize it. Anyway...........pray, pray, pray, not only for John, but for these boys coming in today and for John's buds who are still in Iraq.

Oh! By the way, I received an e-mail from Aaron's mom, Trina (As most of you know, Aaron is John's best bud, who is still in Iraq) was in a 7 humvee that ran over an IED. PRAISE THE LORD, none of them were seriously injured.

69

Trina was able to tell Aaron about John's improved condition. Aaron told Trina to tell me to tell John, "I love you, man." wow.............how heavy is that?

Ok, gotta go.
Love and thanks to all!

From: Connie McClellan
Subject: Update on John
Date: Sat, 7 Oct 2006 08:53:06 -0500

I am ecstatic to report that John got the shunt pulled out of his head last night and they are moving him to the 5th floor. So, he will no longer be in ICU!!! Hallelujah!!!

Also, Jane made him the most fabulous poster board card (full size 2 ft X 18") with a wonderful poem on it and pictures pasted everyway. Anyway, we're supposed to get him to read, so he was reading the card, doing pretty well....stumbled over a few words, but overall he did great!

Today the physical therapist came in to show us how to work with John's extremities so we can get him walking as quickly as possible.

70

Please pray: Thank you, Lord, that you are doing a work in John's extremities and, in the meantime, giving Carl & me the wisdom and patience to work with him on the physical therapy. Thank you that John will be able to read better than ever. Thank you that he will pass his swallow test on Tuesday. And, Lord, Thank you, thank you, thank you so much that he is going to be out of ICU this morning, in Jesus' name. Amen.

They're expecting three new patients in tonight. I don't know their names yet, but God knows who they are. Thank you, Lord, that you are with these soldiers and their families, giving them the peace that surpasses all understanding, and giving the doctors the wisdom they need to do your work, in Jesus' name. Amen.

Love to all!

Connie

The wounded Marines and soldiers were brought to the hospital from the airport in large, ambulance buses that resembled school buses painted white. The buses pulled in the circle drive in front of the hospital and then the injured were carried into the hospital on gurneys.

71

11

October 8, 2006 – October 10, 2006

W e had so many unanswered questions regarding
John's condition. This e-mail to John's doctor
expressed our exact concerns at that time.

From: Connie McClellan
Sent: Mon 10/9/2006 1:45 PM
To: Dr. Armonda
Subject: John McClellan

Hi Dr. Armonda,

John is now on the 5th floor for which we are so
grateful. I'm hoping that you will be able to evaluate
him in the next couple of days. When you do, here
are some of the questions we have so far:

1.) Do you think the problems he's having
swallowing are due to his brain injury or to the
breathing tube, or is there anyway to know?
2.) Do you think the problems he's having with the
left side of his face are a result of the injury to his
brain, or do you think the nerve was severed? Is there

any chance that might correct itself on its own?

3.) If he passes his swallowing test, what other criteria does he need to satisfy for him to go to the VA center for rehabilitation?

4.) In your opinion,, Is the rehabilitation center in Tampa better suited for brain trauma injuries than Wisconsin. Where in Wisconsin is it?

5.) Will the Rehabilitation Center help him with all of his problems (physical, mental, psychological?)

6.) When will they test his eyes & ears to see what we've got?

He was able to walk to the bathroom (with a little help from his friends, of course, as he's still pretty weak). But that makes him a WALKING, talking miracle, not to mention that he wrote his name on a piece of paper along with something about his M-16, So that makes him a walking, talking and WRITING miracle.

73

I'll look forward to hearing back from you at your earliest convenience.

Thanks so much for everything, Doctor.

Sincerely,
Connie McClellan

From: Connie McClellan
Subject: Update on John
Date: Mon, 9 Oct 2006 07:09:52 -0500

Good Morning!

John is now a walking, talking and writing miracle. Yesterday, while Carl and I had gone to grab a bite, John wrote some things down for his nurse. He wrote his name and then began talking about his M-16 gun (definitely a guy thing).

Every day that goes by he does something that we are able to cross off our list of disabilities. Tomorrow, he goes in for another swallow test. I told him he needs to practice really hard, as this is integral to getting the feeding tube out of his nose, which he despises. So please pray:

Lord, thank you, that John will pass his swallow test tomorrow and also that his vocal chord will come back, in Jesus' name. Amen.

74

Then, I have another request. Could you add Dave Leddy to your prayers. Below is an e-mail to me from Dave's mom, Debbie, whom I met in the waiting room yesterday. She is from Chicago. Her son, Dave, arrived two days after John. Debbie arrived shortly thereafter. Please read below and add Dave to your prayer chain.

Yesterday, John's cousin, Lance, came from Philadelphia to see John. He'll be leaving today. John was SO happy to see him. They "cut up" all afternoon which is what they always do when they're together.

That's all for now.

Love to all.

Connie

One day, shortly after John arrived on the 5th floor, he woke up and was upset because he didn't have his gun with him. This really concerned Carl and me as obviously John was confused; however, we soon chalked it up to the "milk of amnesia" as he never mentioned his gun again. It did, though, impress on us how these boys have been trained to keep their guns with them at all times.

Within two days of our arrival on the 5th floor, I met and immediately bonded with Debbie Leddy. Debbie's son, LCpl. Dave Leddy, was injured by an IED explosion in which he lost two fingers and his leg sustained severe injuries along with a subsequent, serious infection. After his arrival to NNMC, Dave went directly to the 5th floor rather than having to spend time in ICU.

Having learned of the miracles that God had performed on John, and realizing how integral the prayers of my e-mail entourage had been, Debbie sent this e-mail to my address book in desperation for the welfare of her son.

From: Debbie Leddy [mailto:debbieleddy@ hotmail.com]
Sent: Mon 10/9/2006 5:51 AM
Subject: LCpl. Dave Leddy

Hello,
My name is Debbie Leddy and my son Lance Corp. Dave Leddy left on 9/11 from Oahu with John McClellan to go to Iraq. My son was injured on Friday 9/29 and ended up in Germany and

Bethesda NNMC with John. Dave has extensive wounds to his left hand and leg and will need extensive surgeries in the next weeks to fix the damage from the IED that hit him. I ask that you please add him to your prayer list. Connie told me about all her friends that have prayed for John and I hope you will add him to your list of people you pray for on a daily basis. The support here is unbelievable. Thank you so much. You are truly angels who walk this earth.

Debbie Leddy

From: Connie McClellan
Subject: OK, time to pray for the boy.....
Date: Tue, 10 Oct 2006 07:13:56 -0500

76

Today is John's second chance to pass the swallow test. Please pray with me: Thank you, Lord, that John will pass his swallow test today, so he can have REAL food and have the feeding tube taken out of his nose, in Jesus' name. Amen.

Yesterday, John didn't seem to be having a very good day. He slept almost the entire day, and didn't talk much. When Carl & I left the hospital, we were both let down, thinking that John had a setback, neurologically. We didn't admit this to each other at the time, but for the first time since his injury, we were both very concerned about John's psychological well being.

Please read the following account of how God helped us at this point in time:
When we had gone to the hospital yesterday for the last time day, I realized I didn't have my cell

phone. Now, keep in mind, I've had a cell phone for at least 6 or 7 years, maybe longer. In that time, I have NEVER lost it, not even once. Anyway, Carl & I were both confident that it would be back at the hotel, so I didn't "wig out" too much about it. When we got to the hotel, IT WASN'T THERE!! Ok, NOW, I'm starting to wig out. So...Carl called my cell phone and... a man answered it and explained it was sitting next to the computer in the waiting room. We asked that he take it to the Corpsman in John's room, so I could retrieve it there.

When I arrived, the Corpsman didn't have my phone, John had it! As I walked toward his bed, he was ferociously punching a bunch of buttons after which he turned the phone around and stuck it in my face. He had taken two pictures of himself with the phone and retrieved them to show me!! I don't even know how to do that! Thank you, Lord, that my fears disappeared right there! John was just fine; he was just tired.

77

When I got back to the hotel, I told Carl the story. He, too, was ecstatic! It was only then, that we shared to each other, how really concerned we had been. I believe God orchestrated that whole chain of events to show us that John was just fine.

Anyway, I wanted to share that with you all....just another touch from the Lord to let us know he is right here with us on this incredible journey.

Tomorrow, they will be surgically inserting the gold weight into John's eyelid to help his eye to close. That will also help him sleep.
 Love to all!
Connie

P.S. I mentioned earlier that Will (the boy who had the IED rock thrown through his left eye and penetrated to the back of his head) is John's roommate. God has done another miracle: Will totally understands everything that is said to him. He still has a tracheotomy, so he can't talk yet, but.. his prognosis is looking good! He of course, has lost sight in his left eye; however, they are optimistic that his right eye is fine. wow..

Thank you so much for your prayers for Will (and, of course, John.)

Love to all,
Connie

78

One day I overheard the doctors giving Will a verbal cognitive test. I followed along to see how I might do on the test. Amazingly, Will did better on the test than I did! *I think Will's going to be okay, either that or I'm in BIG trouble.*

This is the most wonderful, moving e-mail from the mother of one of the boys who was with John when he was shot.

From: Nilda Anes
Sent: Tue 10/10/2006 1:52 PM
To: Connie McClellan
Subject: Re: [E-mail to the Missourian] Injured Marine moved from ICU

Connie:

Oh how the Lord works his miracles!! Praise God!

I sent this e-mail to the newspaper but I got impatient and during my lunch hour, I called information and got the phone number to the hospital and asked for John's room. I spoke to your husband and told him who I was and that the guys sent the following message for him and for your family: they all wanted him (and you all) to know that they miss him very much and that they are praying for him. They heard today that he was in a coma and that he was going to be removed from the ventilator to see how he would do but that they knew that he would be all right because he is a fighter and a true Marine! My son said, "Mom, he is my saw gunner...he was shot right next to me. Sgt. Davidson and I pulled him to safety into the courtyard and applied first aid and prayed and prayed and prayed until help came. Please call him and his family to let them know that we all are thinking of him and are praying that he have a quick recovery. He is with us.

79

Connie, he proceeded to tell me how much they all love each other as brothers and that there is nothing they wouldn't do for each other. He said that your son is a great Marine and you should be very proud...all those guys in Haditha sure are proud of him and want him
to know that!

God Bless you all and I would love to hear his progress.

I will forward these e-mails to Mario .. every once in a while he is able to get on-line or call. I was blessed and surprised by his call this morning...he had a mission with his call...to let John know "the guys" are thinking of him and praying for him. I know they will be relieved to know his miraculous recovery...John (I'm sure) wears those Shamrocks proudly"...lol

God Bless Our Troops!

Love,
Nilda M. Anes
Proud Marine Mom

From: Connie McClellan
Subject: Commandant General Michael W. Hagee and Sergeant Major John L. Estrada
Date: Tue, 10 Oct 2006 14:27:16 -0500

John just received a visit from Commandant General and Mrs. Michael W. Hagee and Sergeant Major John L. Estrada. Commandant Hagee is the top Marine officer in the whole United States; there is no higher. He's the one who sits with the President. Each of these officials gave John these really cool coins. John responded perfectly.

Sergeant Major Estrada just returned from Iraq where he was with the 2-3 Echo Co.
Wow...

Love, Connie

There was never a dull moment on the 5th floor at Bethesda NNMC. If it wasn't something going on with John's dramatic improvements, it was some celebrity or political big wig stopping by to encourage the troops.

Receiving the visit from General and Mrs. Hagee served as one of the true highlights of our time at NNMC. They visited all the soldiers, not just the Marines, and the coins they gave us that day were the first of many we received during our NNMC experience. We learned these coins to be a popular alternative to business cards. John came home with a collection of no less than 20 coins.

Shortly after General Hagee's visit, LCpl. Patrick Howard stopped by our room. LCpl Howard had been a patient at NNMC just a couple of months before we arrived. On July 18, 2006 while serving in Ramadi, Iraq, Patrick had been struck in the chest by two mortar rounds. If he hadn't had the pictures to prove it, I never would have believed the same young man that stood in front of us could have been so severely injured. What encouragement his visit gave to us at a time when we needed it most. We were very grateful that he took the time to visit us.

81

From: Connie McClellan
Subject: Please pray for the family of one of John's Buds.....very sad.
Date: Tue, 10 Oct 2006 4:53 PM

From: Nilda Anes
Sent: Tue 10/10/2006 4:06 PM
To: Connie McClellan
Subject:

Connie:

I am sorry to be the bearer of sad news, but I just wanted you to know that another one of our guys was shot in the head by the sniper on Sunday, but he died. Jeremy Sandvich (Monroe) was in our boys Platoon in Afghanistan but had recently switched to another Platoon while in Iraq. My son, Mario, said that their squad was patrolling and were about 3 blocks away when they heard the gunfire..the sniper shot Sandy in the back of the head and he died instantly.

I met "Sandy" when we went to Hawaii to welcome the plane coming in from Afghanistan in January of this year. I'm sure that John knows him well. I do not know if you want to tell him of his death or not just yet but I do ask for prayer for him and his family..

82

God bless you all and praise God...God's hand was on John as he was saved...his work is not done in this world...what a miracle your son is.

Love,
Nilda

12

October 11, 2006 – October 15, 2006

From: Connie McClellan
Subject: John will go in for his gold weight surgery within the hour
Date: Wed, 11 Oct 2006 08:19 AM

83

Please pray

Lord, in the name of Jesus, we thank you for giving the doctors everything they need to make this procedure successful, and to protect John during the procedure, in Jesus' name. Amen

I told John that not only will this help him to close his left eye, but it will also increase his net worth by about $200..it is gold, you know...lol

Tomorrow, (I think, but you never know for sure on scheduling around here) he should go in for his third swallow test. Please keep him in prayer for that.

Love, Connie

From: Connie McClellan
Subject: John's eye surgery went well
Date: Wed, 11 Oct 2006 14:20:11 -0500

His eye's a little swollen, but the swelling should subside by tomorrow.

Our next obstacle is that swallow test which will take place tomorrow, hopefully in the morning sometime. As I mentioned before, his nose feeding tube will be removed regardless. If he fails the swallow test, they will insert his feeding tube directly into his stomach which will not be uncomfortable for him. I'm good with that, but I would LOVE to see him pass that test!

Love, Connie

84

For John, each day at NNMC consisted of doctors' visits, tests, therapies, sleeping and visitors. Other than the sleeping, the same could be said for Carl and me, except we had the added excitement of things going on outside of John's room...

From: Connie McClellan
Sent: Thu 10/12/2006 9:46 AM
Subject: Just another touch from God...

This is an article from the Presidential Prayer team whom I JUST HAPPENED to meet in the Liaison's office last week. The REALLY wild part about this story is, I was waiting for the shuttle driver to take me to get a rental car. He was looking and looking and looking for the keys to the van which are kept in a special drawer. He looked in the drawer, went to look somewhere else, came back to look in the drawer, went to look somewhere else. This went on for about 15 minutes. That's when the Presidential Prayer team guys came in and introduced themselves to the Liaison officers. I popped out of my couch and blurted, "Presidential Prayer Team!! Oh my gosh! I've been a member with you since practically the beginning in 2001....what you all do is so important.......yaddy, yaddy, yaddy." I went on and on about how great I think they are and so on. In retrospect, I was kind of embarrassed about the way I acted.......almost like a Presidential Prayer Team groupie or something.) Anyway, they were really nice, and asked what I was doing here, so I told them our story............about John.......... about everything that had happened.............and the healing miracles God had worked............. They were like, "WOW...... WHOA ......WOW!" They, too, were in awe of the story I relayed. At that point, they asked, "May we get a picture of you, and then would you e-mail us this story so we can put it in the Presidential Prayer Team newsletter?"

85

I'm like...... "Yes, sirree....you betcha.........let's go.......get the camera", because..... guess what?!?!?!? The Presidential Prayer Team newsletter goes to 100,000 people and they are ALL prayer warriors!" They took a picture of the three of us. I e-mailed them the story, and it was in the next Presidential Prayer Team publication.

Now, any of you who have been in the military know, the first thing they do in training is to train you to put your stuff in the same place, so you'll always know where it is. So, it was EXTREMELY unusual for those van keys to have not been in the drawer. However, had they been in the drawer, I would have been 10 minutes gone from that office and would not have had the encounter with the PPT. Then, after we met, talked, prayed and had the photo shoot, guess what...........the liaison found the van keys!

That, to me, was just example of God's orchestrating power. This whole scenario was just..SOOOOOOO... GOD!!

Love to all,
Connie

From: Connie McClellan
Feeding Tube surgery coming soon
Date: Fri, 13 Oct 2006 07:51:47 -0500

Ok...I'm beginning to wonder if we will EVER have a swallow test again! I'm hearing, it is being postponed until Monday; HOWEVER......yesterday the speech therapist gave John more exercises to strengthen the back of his tongue. This will help him pass the swallow test. So, waiting until Monday, gives him the weekend to "study and prepare", so to speak.

The GOOD news is: He is DEFINITELY scheduled for the feeding tube to be inserted in his stomach and taken OUT OF HIS NOSE! (Thank you, Jesus!! Phew!) He despises that thing in his nose, so this will be a welcomed surgery. As I'm understanding, even if he passes the swallow test and is able to eat, he won't be able to consume enough nutrition by mouth for a while, so with the feeding tube in his stomach, he'll get plenty of nutrition.

More good news! We met with the doctors this morning. They say everything is looking REALLY good for him to leave Bethesda and MORE than likely be transferred to the Rehab Center in Tampa...........in the week to ten days!! Needless to say, we are THRILLED with THAT report!

In the meantime please pray:

Thank you, Lord, that you are continuing your work in John, taking him to that 100% recovery stage. Thank you, that his pain will be gone, that his vocal chords, eyesight, hearing, motor skills, neuro function and everything else will be restored 100%. Thank you for keeping his spirits up and frustrations low, in Jesus' name. Amen.

87

Love to all.
Connie

The feeding tube surgery went well providing a much more comfortable means by which John could be given nourishment. Even if he passed the swallow test, he would still need substantial nourishment, so the feeding tube served as a welcome alternative to the nose tube.

From: Connie McClellan
Subject: A "funny" in the John McClellan story
Date: Sat, 14 Oct 2006 06:41:55 -0500

My new best friend, Debbie Leddy (mother of injured Marine, Dave Leddy, for whom we requested prayer), called her local Schaumburg, IL newspaper to see if they would do a story on Dave. (Debbie, like me, is a strong believer in prayer, and has seen what an important role publicity has had in John's situation in getting thousands of people to pray for his recovery, and is hoping to get a similar prayer response for Dave).

Anyway, the woman at the newspaper said, "Oh yes, I think we received an e-mail about your son. Is his name............John McClellan?" Debbie had to laugh, and then said, "No!! John is on our floor, but my son's name is Dave Leddy!" Soon, the paper is going to do a feature story on Dave, which will be wonderful for letting people know to pray.

Isn't that something?

We are getting cards, letters and e-mails from all over the world. Thank you, WORLD!!

And, get this......our next door neighbor's son, Mike Rawson, works in India and knows the #2 man under the Dahlia Lama. (sp?) Joan, our neighbor, told us that the temples in India were praying for John for an entire day last week. WOW...........

We've gotten word that a big wig is coming in @10:30 this morning. They won't say who it is, so I'll have to get back to you, but for sure, we're going to get John bathed and shaved so he looks his best for whomever!

Never a dull moment; I'll give you that!

Later,

Love, Connie

From: Connie McClellan
Subject: And, the mystery guest was...
Date: Sat, 14 Oct 2006 10:33:02 -0500

Secretary of Defense, Donald Rumsfeld and his wife, Joyce!

FORTUNATELY, John was awake, in spite of the fact that he had to have an extra dose of morphine to overcome the pain resulting from the stomach surgery.

We were able to get a picture of the Rumsfelds with John on the digital. I'll forward as soon as I can get the camera hooked up. Also, the White House photographer took one of John, Carl, Shea, & me with Mr. Rumsfeld. We'll be getting that later. I also had him sign the first Columbia Tribune article, which will be a nice memento.

While he's got the extra dose of pain medication, we're going to take advantage of the situation by trying to raise his bed up and get him used to sitting up. This movement is extremely painful to his head and makes him very dizzy. While he's medicated will be a good time to try and work through the pain and dizziness, which the doctors have assured us is normal.

Later....

Connie

89

Since Debbie and Dave Leddy arrived on the 5th floor a week before us, Debbie had more opportunities to observe a few things. She deduced when a certain plain-clothes security man, whom we nicknamed "Hallcruiser," walked and staked out the floor, it meant someone famous was coming to the floor that day.

Within the first week of our arrival on the 5th floor, Debbie whispered to me, "Hey! I think somebody big's coming up today!"

"Cool! Who is it?"

"I don't know, but I saw Hallcruiser on the floor this morning doing his stakeout thing."

Immediately I went back to the corpsman in John and Will's room. (We always had to have a corpsman in their room, because one time John forgot he couldn't walk and got up to go to the bathroom and fell flat on his face. As a result, the staff made sure a corpsman watched the boys at all times.) I announced to the corpsman, "Hey! I heard someone famous is coming today!"

"Yeah," he replied.

"Who is it?" I asked.

"I can't tell you," he responded.

"Okay...well...on a scale of 1-10, what is he?"

"9.5."

"Dick Cheney? Dick Cheney's coming up?" Immediately, I went all over the floor telling everyone that the Vice President was coming. I went to Debbie and blurted, "Hey, Debbie! Dick Cheney's coming up to 5th!"

She responded, "I just heard it's Donald Rumsfeld."

"Oh!" I exclaimed, and darted back to John's corpsman and nonchalantly stated, "So...I heard Don Rumsfeld's coming up today."

"How'd you know?"

"Ah-ah-ah!! Gotcha!"

Even though number two man, Dick Cheney, wasn't coming, having third in line Donald Rumsfeld was certainly the next best thing. After all, he was the Secretary of Defense...then. For him to visit the floor reminded us how important these Marines and soldiers are to the Defense Department.

Soon after we deduced the identity of the mystery guest, Hallcruiser came by the room and inquired if John would like to meet Mr. Rumsfeld. I asked, "John, would you like to meet Secretary of Defense Rumsfeld?"

John responded wearily, "Oh Mom, I'm just too tired." Disappointed, I advised Hallcruiser this wasn't going to be a good day for John to have company. Of course, had John said, "Yes," I would have had the Corpsman get the razor and shaving cream as, by this time, John looked a tad ratty.

91

About two hours later, Hallcruiser, stopped by the outside of our room and inquired once more, "Are you sure John wouldn't want to meet the Secretary of Defense?"

I responded, "Let me check."

Again I asked John, but this time he replied more excitedly in his weary Marlon Brando voice, "Okay, I'll see him."

I raced back out to the hall to let Hallcruiser know, "He'll see him!! But please apologize to Mr. Rumsfeld that he's not shaven."

92

SEC. OF DEFENSE RUMSFELD "STUDYING UP" OUTSIDE JOHN'S ROOM

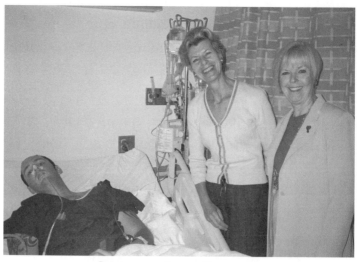

JOHN WITH LYNNE PACE AND FORMER IRAQI AMBASSADORS' WIFE.

Before entering each patient's room, Mr. Rumsfeld did his homework. He stood outside each room studying the respective patient's history. He knew John's name, his hometown, his parents' and sister's names, and other personal information. He knew all about us.

Don and his wife, Joyce were as gracious, appreciative, and compassionate, as we could have hoped. Before he left he gave us one of his personalized coins which we added to our rapidly growing coin collection.

Also during that third week at the Bethesda NNMC, we received a visit from Lynne Pace, the Joint Chief of Staff's wife, who was accompanied by the former Iraqi Ambassador's wife. They were very friendly, attentive and genuinely interested in John's condition, and they expressed their sincere appreciation to John for the sacrifices he had made.

93

From: Connie McClellan
Subject: Urgent prayer needed for Dave Leddy!!!
Date: Sat, 14 Oct 2006 09:00:58 -0500

Dave Leddy has taken a turn for the worse. He's been having nonstop infections due to that Iraqi bacteria. As you will recall, this is the same bacteria for which we had to wear the gowns, gloves and masks when John was in the ICU. Dave has a serious infection in his colon; there is discussion of removing his colon or it could be fatal.

PLEASE pray with me:

Lord, in the name of Jesus, we know it is your desire that Dave is healed TOTALLY of these infections and anything else that's not right. Heal him, Lord. Heal him in the name of Jesus. And, in the meantime, give his family the peace that surpasses all understanding at this difficult, trying time. We trust in your word, Lord, that if we ask anything in your name, that it will be done by our Lord. Amen.

Thank you so much for your prayers.

Love, Connie

From: Carl & Rhonda Smith
Sent: Sun 10/15/2006 8:03 PM
To: Connie McClellan
Subject: Wishing John a Speedy and Full Recovery

94

Mr. & Mrs. McClellan,

Please let us introduce ourselves, we are Carl and Rhonda Smith. Our son LCpl. Trent Smith serves with your son as a machine gunner with E 2/3. Trent roomed with John upon their return from Afghanistan. I believe that you may have met Trent this past summer, as it is our understanding that you visited K-Bay. Trent has always spoken very highly of John.

I hope that it is o.k. for us to contact you in this way. My ex-sister-in-law, Gail Moore lives in Columbia and has a friend (Marti) that I believe works for Mr. McClellan. I had contacted Gail and had asked

for any updates she could provide for us on John's condition so that
I could forward that information to Trent in Haditha. She had forwarded to us an e-mail from Marti that had your e-mail address.

We wish you peace and comfort during this time. Please pass on our well wishes to LCpl. John.

Sincerely,

Carl & Rhonda Smith

This, to me, was another "Godsidence." The 'Marti' about whom Carl Smith spoke was not only someone we knew, but two days before we received his e-mail, my husband hired Marti (via long distance telephone)! What a Godsidence that was! God was letting us know, "I'm still here; I will not leave you or forsake you."

95

13

October 16, 2006 – October 19, 2006

96

From: Connie McClellan
Date: October 16, 2006
Subject: E-mail from John's commanding officer in Iraq

This is an e-mail from Capt. Matthew Tracy, who is John's commanding officer. It is to Maj Wood, who was here to visit John yesterday. This is a fabulous testament to John's Company (Echo Co.). I thought you all would appreciate the accolades (and enthusiasm). Love, Connie

Sent: Sun 10/15/2006 3:44 PM
To: Connie McClellan
Subject: Fw: SITREP FROM MAJ WOOD -- LCPL LEDDY SLEEPING

From: Tracy Capt Matthew W (GCE RCT-7 2/3 ECHO CO COMMANDER)
Sent: Wednesday, October 11, 2006 4:19:32 PM
Subject: RE: SITREP FROM MAJ WOOD -- LCPL LEDDY SLEEPING

Sir,

Great to hear from you. It is awesome here. Echo Co is a total machine. They love it and can't wait for the next patrol. We have built a fantastic team IP, IA, CAG, Echo, HET all are dedicated. All the weak sisters are quiet or are hiding at the Dam because it is hot in the kitchen. The Marines are sooooo good. I'd never have even dreamed these NCOs could be this good. You would be so proud. Don't believe any b.s. about high casualties because Marines are "learning." At least not in Echo. The difference between MV and now week three is like night and day. They are hungry, savage and very smart.
Matt

From: Connie McClellan
Date: October 16, 2006
Subject: Miraculous News on Dave Leddy

97

I just talked to Debbie Leddy. If, what has happened to John, does not make you believe in miracles, read this:

Yesterday morning Dave's white count was 28,000. Yesterday afternoon, it was 17000. I'm not sure what normal is, but I know it's not 17000. ANYWAY, today his white count is normal and his temperature is normal and his heart rate is normal. All of these were exceptionally elevated yesterday. His temperature was over 103! We are REELING WITH JOY!!

Thank you SOOOOOOOO much for your prayers. God has been VERY busy (in a great way) here at Bethesda National Naval Medical Center!!
Love, Connie

From: Connie McClellan
Date: 10/16/06
Subject: John sat up in a chair today

John sat up in a chair today. It was tough early on as he was spinning like crazy, but he hung in there and stayed in the chair for almost an hour, which was incredible. John received two calls from his buds in Iraq today. He was so happy to talk to them. Anyway, that's all for now.
Love to all!
Connie

From: Connie McClellan
Subject: E-mail from John's Company Commander
Date: Tue, 17 Oct 2006 06:19:57 -0500
If this doesn't make you "well" up...

98

This is an e-mail from John's Company Commander, Capt. Matthew Tracy.

From: Tracy Capt Matthew W (GCE RCT-7 2/3 ECHO CO COMMANDER)
Sent: Tue 10/17/2006 1:13 AM
To: Connie McClellan
Subject: John McClellan Our Motivator

Connie,
My name is Capt Matthew Tracy. I am John's Company Commander, Echo Company CO. Major Wood asked me to send some more news to John. I will make arrangements for some of the members of the squad to give John a call. We are thinking of him quite a bit and miss him dearly. He is very

popular in the platoon and everyone is hoping for a full recovery. A woman named Kathy Levy sent us an article about your candlelight vigil and the miracle that occurred. We have it posted where we form up before we go on patrol. Having been standing there when we put John on the Helo I can testify that it is plain evidence to me of the power and glory of God. We all thought he was gone. His recovery has been an inspiration to us all out here.

The Company continues to bring the Heavy Metal in an unrelenting fashion. With a total disregard for pain and fatigue Echo Company continues to hunt, especially the Marines of 1st Platoon. Who were engaged in their first sustained firefight just a couple of days ago as Cpl Carson and Sgt Ciotola drove unmercifully through a far ambush in the Palm Groves. They performed beautifully. Numerous and different sources indicate the enemy does not like the new unit in town.

99

John - take care and get well.
Sincerely,
Matt Tracy

I didn't realize how comforting my e-mails were to some of the other military parents. Hearing about the miracles God did for John helped to strengthen their faith by reminding them that God heard and answered our prayers and will do the same for them.

From: Nilda Anes
Sent: Tue 10/17/2006 2:21 PM
To: Connie McClellan
Subject: Praise the Lord for what he has done for John

Connie:

Every day that I receive an e-mail on John, I thank God for His healing hand. I was talking with some of my fellow MOMS (mothers of military soldiers) and they were commenting on how wonderful and miraculous it is that he is alive and will recover..one Mom said what if his head would have been turned an inch or half an inch to one side or other!? John's recovery is truly a miracle, and I thank God every time I think of it...

I know all this is trying on you but I am impressed and amazed at your strength..spiritual, physical and emotional. I pray that God continues to give you all three...

Please tell John that I am so very proud of him and tell him I said to be strong, hang in there and an entire nation thanks him for a job well done!

I read the e-mail from Capt Matthew Tracy and John's toughness and survival is what has pumped that company up...everything they are doing is with John in mind..Mario said they have John's picture posted sporting a "thumbs up"..

Finally, thank you for keeping me informed.. actually for keeping me, my family and our

MOMS group informed here in South Texas! GOD CONTINUE TO BLESS YOU ALL!!

Love,
Nilda

From: Connie McClellan
Date: 10/18/2006
Subject: Visitors today...

Today, John received a visit from two of the Rockets!! That got a smile out of him! In fact, he's been smiling a LOT today, so that has been the big news for today!

At the moment, he's getting that long, overdue shave.

No word on the swallow reschedule - we're still trying to keep him elevated as much as possible, so that when it does happen, he'll be ready.

I spoke with his doctor, he said he doesn't have to pass the swallow test before he goes to Tampa; they can do it there anytime. So.....no pressure....I like it!

Later.

Love to all,
Connie

From: Connie McClellan
Subject: Pictures of John with Presentation of
Third Purple Heart by General Michael Hagee
Date: Thu, 19 Oct 2006 12:22:50 -0500

General Michael Hagee was in just a few minutes ago to present John with his 3rd purple heart. This medal is the same as his first and second, except it has 2 stars on it, each representing a purple heart + the purple heart medal = 3.

General Hagee told John that he is only the 2nd Marine General Hagee has met that has received 3 purple hearts. The first was a soldier from the Vietnam era.

It was a proud moment for us all.
Love, Connie

102

From: Connie McClellan
Thursday, October 19, 2006
CORRECTION..........

John received a visit yesterday from two ROCKETTES, not Rockets, not that he doesn't appreciate professional sports, but there's a HUGE difference between a Rockette & a Rocket......lol

He had a GREAT sleep last night. The staff is now under orders to not awaken him for anything from 10PM to 6AM. Sleep is so critical to brain injury recovery, so that is excellent. He's still sleeping now.

If anyone has any good (not raunchy, please) jokes, would you pass them on? Someone sent him a couple of jokes and REALLY made him smile, so I'll pass any along that come through.

More later,
Love, Connie

At this point, John had experienced little joy, so getting him to smile rated high on our list of priorities. He'd had a few smiles, but they were few and far between. Hundreds of e-mailed jokes had prompted a few feeble grins, but his true joy had yet to return. And, of course, with the facial nerve severed, the few smiles we witnessed were severely lopsided.

From: Connie McClellan
Sent: Fri 10/20/2006 2:04 PM
Subject: And the celebrity guest today was......

Anthony Swofford!!

Who's that, you ask? (I had to ask that myself.... we don't get to the movies much...lol)

He is the author and star of the book and movie, Jarhead. He autographed the book for John, so I'm anxious to start reading it to him. Then, we'll have a better appreciation of the fact that he came to visit. He's a very nice guy.

Later...
Love to all, Connie

103

FROM: Connie McClellan
SENT: 10/20/2006   4:10 PM
CORRECTION...................

Ok, ok, so he's not the star of the movie (I just got the rest of the story). Anthony Swofford is the author about whom the book was written and the movie based.
Sorry for the error.

Love, Connie

After John's tenth day on the 5th floor, Carl bought John some Old Spice stick deodorant. Carl removed the cap and handed the deodorant to John. John held it with his right hand, but his left hand, which at this point had limited function, began a rapidly pulling movement on top of the deodorant. Carl and I looked at each other. *What is he doing?* Then, all of a sudden, John pulled a safety cap off the top of the container. With much chagrin, Carl & I realized the deodorant had two caps. We immediately burst out laughing! *Who* has had the brain trauma here? Obviously John knew what he was doing, but we, on the other hand, had NOT a clue!

Throughout his time at NNMC, John experienced severe headaches and dizziness, especially when he tried to sit up. One day I told him, "John, I know exactly how you feel with the head spinning thing. When I was 14 years old, a classmate, Renee Riutzel, had a sleepover. Someone brought a 6-pack of beer which we all drank. My head was spinning like crazy! It was *horrible*! That happened a long time ago, but I will *never* forget it. I really *do* know how you feel."

That afternoon, I received an e-mail from… *Renee Riutzel*! This was just… *so*.. God, as Renee and I really weren't even that close growing up; in fact, I'm not sure I had even talked to her since that night when I had too much to drink at her house some forty years ago! Immediately, I wrote her back, "You're not going to believe this! I was *just* talking about you this morning!"

Then, two weeks later, two hours after relaying the Renee Riutzel story to a friend, I received *another* e-mail from Renee! I couldn't believe it! In this coincidental way, again, God again reminded me, "I'm still here; I will not leave you or forsake you."

105

14

October 20, 2006 – October 23, 2006

Persuading John to sit up presented us one of our biggest challenges during our days at NNMC. Because of the immense discomfort he experienced with even a small degree of elevation, John strongly resisted any sitting up opportunities.

From: Connie McClellan
Subject: Ok.....it's time.....please pray
Date: Fri, 20 Oct 2006 11:01 AM

It's time to get John sitting up. He's been very resistant because it's painful and nauseating; however, as I've mentioned before, the only way he's going to get through the pain is to sit up and eventually the symptoms will subside. So, they're going to give him some pain medication and anti-nausea medication, so we can try to get past this hurdle.

My goal is to have him sitting up and in a wheelchair in time for tomorrow night's World Series St.

Louis Cardinals'/Detroit Tigers game where he can watch it in the lounge area with a big screen. GO CARDS!!

Last night we watched the first 1 3/4 hours of the game on TV. This was the first time John has wanted to watch TV, so that was another huge step forward. He was then ready to go to sleep (as were we,.so his timing was good).

Anyway, please pray: Thank you, Lord, that John will be able to tolerate sitting up and staying up without being nauseated and without head pain. And, thank you, Lord, that headaches will NOT plague him as a result of his injuries, in Jesus' name. Amen.

Later....
Love to all, Connie

On October 20th, Carl, John, and I were in John's room, when a policeman entered the room. "Hi," the man greeted in the most pronounced Brooklyn accent I'd ever heard. "My name's Bobby, and I'm a friend of a friend of Jamie and Sonya's in Florida."

Jamie, my nephew, and his wife Sonya lived in Florida. This was a friend of a friend of theirs? Talking to the three of us, Bobby continued, "I just want you to know my wife and I live ten minutes away, and we are here for you." Facing Carl and me he continued, "I have Sundays off, and we would love to have you over for dinner." Addressing John, he said, "John, I am so proud of you. Thank you for everything you have done; I appreciate it so much. Whatever I can do to make you more comfortable, just say the word." At that moment, he presented John a coin, which was the most beautiful of all the coins John had received.

I exclaimed, "Oh, Bobby, this is the most beautiful of all the coins that we've been given!"

He responded, "This coin has value; I'm with the Metropolitan Police Dept! If you ever have a problem, you show them this coin, and you won't have a problem anymore."

We all laughed.

We discussed what would we do to display all the coins John had received. Bobby relayed, "Yeah my brother's a Marine, and I'm in the Navy. My brother gives me a bunch of crap about me being in the Navy. He's always giving me a bunch of Marine stuff. A couple of years ago, he gave me one of those coin racks with the Marine emblem on it." Again, we all laughed.

Suddenly, he blurted, "Well, gotta go!" At that point, he leaned over and gave John a kiss on the cheek, turned around, and I saw that Bobby was...crying! It was one of the most touching displays of compassion I'd ever witnessed.

The next day, here Bobby came with a plastic bag under his arm. Out of the bag, he produced the Marine coin rack his brother had given him. "I didn't want to commit to it yesterday, 'cause I wanted to check with my brother to make sure it was okay with him. He said it was okay." At that point, he presented John the coin rack.

Bobby reiterated, "Now, I'm serious, I've got Sundays off; if you want to come over for dinner, my wife and I... we'd *love* to have you."

I suggested, "Well, Carl is leaving to go back to Columbia, but my nephews from Chicago and Philadelphia are coming to see John on Sunday. Maybe the three of us could come for dinner. How about I give you a call Sunday morning?"

"Oh," he responded excitedly, "Gimme a call, gimme a call!"

That Sunday, my nephews Lance and Larry Loethen arrived. Almost immediately after they walked into John's room, Larry, who is an Edward Jones Representative, announced, "John, in July, Edward Jones is taking you and me on a trip!" Larry then presented John with a brochure of fourteen available trips and declared, "And you're going to pick the place!" John smiled the biggest, albeit lopsided, smile we'd seen since his injury. He was elated, not only at the prospect of going on a great trip, but also of going with these cousins, with whom he loved spending time.

109

Of course, up to now, John had only sat up once, and hadn't walked at all, so I had to continually encourage myself, *"This is October. July is nine months away...He WILL be able to do this!"*

Due the headaches, nausea and head spinning, we

had a tremendous amount of difficulty persuading John to get up into a wheelchair and go outside. However, in order to get past the symptoms, he would have to force himself to sit up. Knowing how much John loved and respected his cousins, I pulled them aside and suggested, "Guys, we have to get him to sit up. See if he'll climb into the wheelchair and go outside with you."

Lance took the lead, "Hey John! What do you say we go outside?"

"Sure," John responded weakly.

"All right!" I exclaimed. "You guys need to stay here forever! He'll do anything for you!"

We maneuvered John into the wheelchair and rolled him outside for the first time. By that time it was about 4:00 in the afternoon and chilly. Even though we anticipated the cool temperature and bundled John in blankets, we only stayed long enough for me to take a picture of the cousins together. Even though the trip was brief, it allowed John to cross the threshold to overcoming the pain, nausea and head spinning. By the time we arrived back to his room, he was totally exhausted; all he wanted was to take a nap.

I suggested, "You take a nap, while we go to Bobby's for dinner and then when we come back, we'll move you into the wheelchair and down to the day room. You don't want to miss watching the Cardinals beat Detroit in the World Series! How's that sound?"

"Okay," he responded weakly.

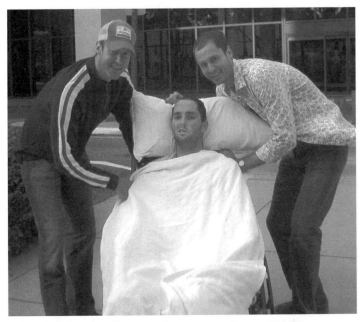

JOHN WITH COUSINS, LANCE AND LARRY LOETHEN

Lance, Larry, and I returned to the hotel and phoned Bobby, who immediately drove to our hotel, picked us up, and took us to his home, where we were welcomed by his wife, Lore. Lore and Bobby offered us a smorgasbord of brats, appetizers, beer, wine, and bread. Then, in walked all of their neighbors, friends, and family to honor John by way of us. It was an incredible experience.

After dinner, Bobby drove us back to the hospital and pulled into the circle drive so he could go up with us and say goodnight to John. I stopped him, "Oh, Bobby, we can't park here. These parking places are for the ambulance buses and big wigs. We'll need to go to the parking garage and then we can walk over on the bridge." Bobby threw this emblem-like patch on the dash and retorted, "Didn't I tell you I'm with the Metropolitan Police Department?" I laughed. "Yes, as a matter of fact you did."

So, we parked in that circle drive and didn't get in any trouble at all! After visiting with John, Bobby gave me one of those emblems, and explained, "Now if you ever have any problem finding a parking spot, you just put this on the dash of your car."

"All righty then!" We laughed!

We wanted to get John in the wheelchair and take him to the day room to watch the World Series, but he was still too exhausted from our earlier outdoor trek. So, we tucked him in for the night and then Lance, Larry, and I walked back to the hotel and watched the Cardinals' World Series victory over Detroit.

112

Afterwards, I called my sister, Marilyn, in Florida and relayed the great time we had with Bobby, a friend of a friend of (her son) Jamie and Sonya's.

"Oh! That's so great!" she replied.

The next day Marilyn called back. "Jamie and Sonya are trying to figure out who Bobby is a friend of!"

That's how remote the "Bobby" relationship was! This was a perfect example of the outpouring of compassion that continually blessed us throughout our experience. People we didn't even know were loving us, praying for us, doing for us, and just... always there for us.

On the afternoon of October 21st, John's nurse overfilled his feeding tube causing John to vomit followed by a severe coughing and gagging spell. As a precaution, he had a chest x-ray to be sure nothing had spilled into his lungs. His lungs were clear, but in the x-ray, they noted a small hole underneath his diaphragm. Immediately, I sent an e-mail requesting prayer for this condition. Soon after a follow up examination, the doctors found that the hole had disappeared, documenting another miracle for our record book.

From: Connie McClellan
Date: October 22, 2006 11:20 AM
Subject: John's left eye

Just this morning, John's left lower eye is kind of drooping (from underneath, due probably to the absence of muscle action) which is making his left eye not quite close again.

113

Please pray with me:

Thank you, Lord, in the name of Jesus that you are healing the left side of John's face, not just his drooping eye, but the entire left side of his face! In the name of Jesus, WE WILL NOT HAVE TO DEAL WITH THIS SEMI-CLOSED EYE DILEMMA! The Bible says "By his stripes, John HAS (Isaiah 53:5) and IS (1 Peter 2:24) healed. Let this be a continued witness, Lord, to the thousands that have been touched by John's story. Let the world continue to know, that You are STILL in the miracle working business. You have said in Your Word, Lord, "If two or more of you agree about anything you ask for, it will be done for you by my Father in heaven. Where two or three come together in my name, there am I with them." Thank you for your Word, Lord. And thank you as you have said in Isaiah 55.11: "So is my word that goes out from my mouth: It will not return to me empty, but will accomplish what I desire and achieve the purpose for which I sent it." We know it is your desire that John be made whole, Lord. DO IT, in Jesus' name. Amen

Thank you SOOOOOOOO much for your prayer support!

Love to all, Connie

114

From: Connie McClellan
Subject: This if from John's First Plt
Commander - good news, but also sad news
Date: Sun, 22 Oct 2006 12:05:53 -0500

Please pray: Thank you, Lord, that you are with the families of Sandy and Josh. Give them your peace that can only come from You at such a devastating time as this, in Jesus' name. Amen.

From: David Kelm Sent: Sun 10/22/2006
11:46 AM
To: Connie McClellan
Subject: Just Keeping In Touch

Mrs. McClellan,

My dad's been forwarding me a lot of e-mails

and pictures of John. It's great to see how well he's doing. Please keep sending the updates; as you can imagine, there are a lot of guys around here that are very interested in how he's doing.

Things continue to go well here. The new Iraqi Police force, although small right now, is worth their weight in gold. The enemy is reeling, and we're seeing results. We have taken over 200 detainees in just a month. The locals are in love with us, and can't figure out how polite and respectful we are to them, but how ruthless we are to the insurgents. We do, of course, continue to have our bad days. The sniper out here is good. Several Marines have been hit in the Kevlar or had very near misses. We have also lost two Marines, LCpl Jeremy Sandvick Monroe, and 2ⁿᵈ Lt Josh Booth, to the sniper. I pray everyday, and I thank God for sparing John that day.

115

But, all things considered, we are winning here in Haditha, and John's friends are doing well and continue to ask about him. I'm going to take those pictures to 1ˢᵗ Sgt Atkins in the morning and make sure they're printed out for all to see. Again, if there is anything that I or my friends in the DC area can do for you, *anything at all*, please don't hesitate to let me know. You're family, after all.

-Dave Kelm, 1st Plt Cmdr

Subject: FW: LCpl McClellan
Date: Mon, 23 Oct 2006 06:52:16 -0500
Atkins 1stSgt Darryl L Sent: Mon 10/23/2006
1:44 AM
To: Connie McClellan
Subject: LCpl McClellan
Classification: UNCLASSIFIED

Mrs. McClellan,

116

Just received your e-mail address and wanted to send a shout out to John and the rest of your family. We are excited to hear that he is improving at a rapid rate. God is good. You know how things are. We hear snippets of how good his health is. I'd rather hear it from you. How is he doing, really? I want to be able to brief to the rest of the staff and get the word back to the Marines. I received a letter from a young woman from Michigan about what happened to John (she was concerned and wanted to show her support) and she sent me an e-mail excerpt showing how well he was doing and how he was improving. It's amazing to get stuff from across the country.

Let John know the company is kicking ass. Period. We are in the toughest area for our battalion and the Marines here are doing heroic things on a daily basis. I see young warriors doing amazing things daily. Let him know that his platoon is doing an outstanding job and they miss him. I've posted a picture of him giving a thumbs up from his hospital bed on our read board. Marines look at him for inspiration before going on patrol. On a sad note, if he's up to it, let him know that we lost two Marines, LCpl Sandvick Monroe and Lt Booth.

Let him know that we will continue to push on and we will hold those responsible, accountable for their actions.

If there is anything that the men of Echo Company can do to assist you, don't hesitate to let me know.

1stSgt D. L. Atkins
Echo Company
2nd Bn 3rd Marines
Hadítha City, Iraq

"Somewhere a True Believer is training to kill you. He is training with minimal food or water, in austere conditions, training day and night. The only thing clean on him is his weapon and he made his web gear. He doesn't worry about what workout to do - his ruck weighs what it weighs, his runs end when the enemy, his competitor, stops chasing him. This True Believer is not concerned about 'how hard it is;' he knows either he wins or dies. He doesn't go home at 17:00, he is home. He knows only The Cause." - anonymous quote

117

From: Connie McClellan
Subject: HE PASSED!!!!
Date: Mon, 23 Oct 2006 15:36:06 -0500

John passed the swallow study!! Hallaluia, it is FINALLY DONE!!

He can now eat ANYTHING he wants....NOT just soft stuff. He's pretty worn out at this time, so he's resting, but once he wakes up and starts to get hungry......the sky's the limit. Thank you, Lord!!!

The only thing we have to watch is thin liquids such as water or broth. He can only take small sips and has to tuck in his chin, so that he doesn't aspirate.

Thank you so much for your prayers!!

Love, Connie

15

October 24, 2006 – October 25, 2006

Rapidly, we approached the time for us to leave Bethesda for rehabilitation at the James Haley Veterans Hospital in Tampa, Florida. We kept hearing that it could be any day that we would be making the flight, and then *finally*, on October 24th, we received  word that we would be leaving the next day for Tampa.

Also, on the 24th, Carl flew back to Columbia with the five hand-sewn quilts John received during his stay at NNMC, since they were bulky and we were going to sunny Tampa. These quilts were made by ladies from all over the country who sent them to NNMC and Landstuhl to be given to the wounded Marines and soldiers. One quilt accompanied John on the flight from Germany, but the others, including the Quilt of Valor, were given to him at different times during our stay at NNMC.

Having received the final word that we were heading to Tampa, our instructions were, "Other than your luggage, the only things you'll need are snacks and a blanket, because the plane is cold."

Oh man... I just sent all those blankets with Carl!

So, I walked down to the Marine Liaison's office and inquired, "Oh guys, is there any way I can have another blanket? I just sent all the blankets home with Carl before I realized I would need one for the plane."

"Sure," they replied, as they escorted me to the back room where they had at least fifty quilts neatly piled, and allowed me to hand pick one .

After returning from the Liaison's office, I walked into John's room. On his bed was a hand crocheted, green blanket. *Oh my gosh! Someone must have heard we're going to Tampa and need a blanket!* Noooooooooooooooooo...At the precise time I was downstairs picking out a blanket, volunteers were delivering hand crocheted blankets to all the Marines and soldiers on the floor. Again I had been blessed with another "I'm still here, I will not leave you or forsake you" Godsidence.

120

From: Connie McClellan
Subject: John ate MY pizza!!
Date: Tue, 24 Oct 2006 15:08:31 -0500

Last week, I bought a couple of mini pizzas that I put in our freezer at the hotel. Since we're leaving tomorrow, I'm trying to clean out the frig, so I brought them in and thought I'd have pizza for lunch and dinner. I heated one up, brought it into John's room, and asked if he wanted a bite. Ha! A bite? ? He ate the whole thing! I asked if he wanted me to heat the second one and he said, "Yes, please." (At least he was polite about it...lol). So, I heated that one and he ate 3/4 of it!! (Actually, I act like I'm complaining, but in reality, I was elated!!). Don't worry, I've managed to get plenty to eat...ha!

Also, today, John walked, with a little help from his nursing staff friends, to the bathroom and took a shower! Very cool! (or should I say...Very Warm!) Later, Ronan Tynan the Irish Tenor came by and gave John a CD and wished him well. He said that at the age of 20 he was in a motorcycle accident and lost both legs. Then he went on to become an orthopedic surgeon. Now he sings and travels around the country...SUPER nice guy. He said something about singing the National Anthem at one of the World Series games, but I'm not sure which one or if it has occurred yet. I'll have to get back to you on that one.

121

Also, Bob Woodruff, the ABC journalist who was severely injured in Iraq, was visiting here today. After he was injured in January 2006, he was a patient right down the hall from John's room. Woodruff is writing a book and they're also producing a documentary about his experience. I think they're planning to release it in the Spring. John and I were supposed to be featured in his documentary, but sadly, they're filming tomorrow when John and I will be flying out., So they're going to feature our roommate, Will, instead......
very cool

Love to all, Connie

16

October 25, 2006 – October 30, 2006

Finally, we made it to Tampa. Fortunately, the flight only took about six hours as opposed to the ten hour estimate we were originally given.

From: Connie McClellan
Subject: We made it to Tampa - no worries!
Date: Wed, 25 Oct 2006 9:05 PM

The plane ride wasn't as long as we were originally told (Praise the Lord!).

We left Bethesda National @ 8:00 for Andrews Air Force Base, which is where Air Force One is hangered. This base is BEAUTIFUL and very well maintained. We flew out of Andrews @ about 10:15 AM and proceeded on to Cherry Hill, NC, Ft. Poke, NC and then on to Augusta, GA. John made the trip just fine. There were about 5 other men on gurneys, and about 8 other military men seated. John was the only patient between Augusta and Tampa. He felt very special because he had about 8 people taking care of him. The plane was a C130 Cargo type plane. It looked just like the ones from the '50's but was actually built in 1992. It was pretty cold, but we had blankets. I actually MUCH preferred it to a commercial airplane because:

1.) They served lunch
2.) The lunch was GOOD
3.) I had PLENTY of leg room

We arrived at the airport about 5:30 and got to the VA about 6:30 (Tampa traffic is not AS bad as MD, but still pretty bad). We were met at the airport by the Marine Liaison, and then ambulance arrived shortly thereafter. I rode in the ambulance with John and the Liaison and 2 other military people followed us to the hospital where they waited for me to get John situated ant then delivered me to my hotel. They are wonderful! I'm staying at the Double Tree and it is ABSOLUTELY beautiful and about 1/2 mile from the hospital. They have a computer in the lobby, so that will help me to keep you updated as I don't think I'll be getting a laptop loaner here like I did in Bethesda, and my laptop still is not fixed.

123

I got John all settled into the hospital. He will be evaluated by all teams tomorrow and then moved to the Rehab floor probably on Thursday or Friday.

I hope to have MUCH more news on John tomorrow evening.

Love to all.
Connie

I'll fly a C-130 ANYTIME! I thoroughly enjoyed the experience. John, on the other hand, didn't like it very well, as he was horizontal, strapped in, and all in all, pretty miserable; however better days were just around the corner.

From: Connie McClellan
Subject: HUGE DAY IN TAMPA, FL!
Date: Thu, 26 Oct 2006 1:56 PM

Hi Everyone!

This afternoon John moved to the rehab floor. It's just 2:30 now and already, he's using a walker! That is SO HUGE! He met with the Speech Pathologist this morning and the Physical Therapist and Occupational Therapist this afternoon. So...needless to say, at this moment, he is SOUND asleep...talk about exhausted! But they all marveled at how well he's doing.

Tomorrow, he will start the rehab regimen in ALL departments. He is doing FABULOUS! They'll be able to give me a timetable on Tuesday. They all "pow-wow" on Tuesdays to compile all of the data from the various depts.

That's all for the moment. Thankfully, 2nd floor waiting room has nice, FAST computers, so hopefully I'll be able to touch base as things happen, which at the rate he's going will to be regularly!

One bit of disappointing news, although it's not a big deal: John weighs 172.8 lbs. (When he left, he

124

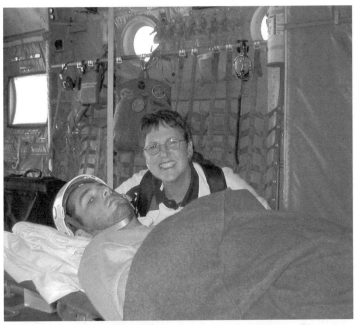

John and Mom on C-130 headed to Tampa, FL

125

John being carried off the C-130
upon arrival at Tampa, FL

weighed 220#). It's no wonder he's so weak. This is the first time they've weighed him since he's been to the states. So, we've got some work to do before they can take out that feeding tube. He has to eat enough to keep his caloric intake up. At this point, he's eating a little more all the time, but still needs the supplements. I estimate it will be at least a week to 10 days before they can take that feeding tube out.

What a great day this has been!

Love, Connie

126

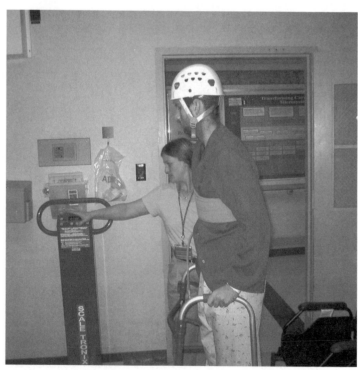

JOHN'S FIRST TIME VERTICAL AND WALKING,
GETTING READY TO GET ON SCALE.

One especially disappointing aspect of John weighing in at 172 lbs was that he only weighed one pound more than me! I learned early on, living out of a hotel was not conducive to healthy eating.

From: Connie McClellan
Subject: Speech Therapy & ENT docs
Date: Fri, 27 Oct 2006 1:27 PM

It's been a big day with therapies. John and I are both exhausted, so he's taking a rest, and I'm getting ready to. He did SO well on his cognitive test with the speech therapist.

We just got back from the ENT doctor. Currently, he has no hearing in his left ear. They're going to do a CT scan to determine the damage to the nerve. We'll, hopefully, know that next week.

Please pray: Thank you, Lord, in the name of Jesus that John's hearing will be restored in his left ear. Amen.

Later.
Love to all,
Connie

127

From: Connie McClellan
Subject: Good food here in Tampa
Date: Sat, 28 Oct 2006 06:03 AM

This morning the speech therapist came in and was going through the cognitive portion of John's testing. As she was going through the paperwork and asking John the appropriate questions, she finally looked at him and said, "I've tried, and

I just can't find any deficiencies." Go ahead... MAKE MY DAY! I was elated!

At 10:00 this morning, John had physical therapy. From the time he got to the gym until he left, he made so much progress with standing and walking. I couldn't believe how much he improved in 45 minutes!

So far the hospital food is not so hot. Fortunately, there are many good restaurants within walking distance. And that allows me to get some exercise as most of the things that he likes are not exactly low in calories. And I certainly wouldn't have him eat alone...that just wouldn't be right...ha!
This afternoon, John's nurse gave him his first real shower.

I met a young soldier in the day room. Last August, while on leave from Iraq, he and his friends thought it would be fun to go fishing...using a grenade. Sadly, before he could throw the grenade into the water, it exploded causing the loss of his right hand. He also suffered EXTREME brain trauma. He seems to be doing pretty well cognitively... fortunately. Please keep him in your prayers. His name is Dave.

Love, Connie

The doctors and staff marveled at the progress John made with his walking during our first week in Tampa. The day after we arrived, he walked 80 steps with his walker, and he increased that to 150 steps within two days. Each day, with extreme exertion, he improved his distance, strength and endurance, but by the time 3:00 PM rolled around, he was absolutely exhausted. So for the first week in Tampa, he spent the afternoons and evenings sleeping.

129

17

October 31, 2006 – November 1, 2006

130

Every day John worked from 8:00 AM to 3:00 PM in his various therapies, which proved to be physically and mentally grueling. Physical therapy tapped every ounce of physical energy he could muster, whereas Speech, Occupational and Recreational therapies resulted in immense mental exhaustion. However, in all areas he had the determination to do whatever he needed to improve as quickly as possible, especially in the area of walking.

From: Connie McClellan
Subject: Yesterday was good but
EXHAUSTING (for all of us)!
Date: Tue, 31 Oct 2006 07:03 AM

Good morning!
They told us to be ready, that yesterday was going to be physically exhausting. That was no joke!

At 8:00, Occupational Therapy came in and worked with John to help him shower and shave. (No more of that Grizzly Adams look...woohoo!). He did great. Other than helping him in and out, he did it all... all by himself!

Then, he had physical therapy and walked 200 steps with the walker, along with a lot of other exercises. This was tiring as his legs are still very weak.

When he's doing his physical therapy sometimes the tube drops down and I tease him that he's dragging his tail between his legs....lol. Needless to say, he'll be glad when we can stop THAT joke...

Then onto Speech Therapy and Vocational Rehabilitation, both of which were kind of boring, which only added to his tiredness.

131

By the end of the day, we were BOTH exhausted. Coming back from Voc Rehab, all John could talk about was taking a nap. So, we got him all settled in his bed....and then here comes the psychologist to take him to Group Therapy which is not optional. He was NOT happy.

But I WAS! He got out of bed and off on his way, and I got INTO his bed pulled up the covers and had a 45 minute POWER NAP. You'll be glad to know, those hospital beds are SOOOOOOOOOOO comfortable.

Later I was talking to one of the other Marines, a double amputee, who didn't know me at the time. He asked me, "Didn't I see you sleeping in one of the beds?"

"Yes"

"Yeah, I wheeled by your room and looked in there and was cussing you, asking my mom, 'Why doesn't she have to go to the *%#*%! GROUP THERAPY!?' "

TOO FUNNY! (As you may have surmised, some of the boys aren't that hot on the group therapy. For one thing, there are only four young soldiers, the rest are much...I mean MUCH older!)

One good thing to come from the group session (other than my power nap, that is) is when John came back he said, "I AM so lucky." I asked what he meant. He said the other (3 younger) soldiers are SO much worse off than he is; it made him really appreciate where he is in relation to where he could be.

132

Hey... I wanted to tell you all, the Head Nurse on the rehab floor is from Columbia. She went to Hickman H.S. until she was a Junior. Her name then was Marti Lambeth. She would have been with the graduating class of '62. Anybody know her? She is SUPER nice, as are ALL of the nurses on the floor. I am very impressed with this facility, except, maybe...for the food....ha!

Please pray: Thank you, Lord, that today John will see more progress, and be encouraged by it, and not as worn out. Thank you, again, Lord, that you are restoring him completely in Jesus' name. Amen.

Love you guys!
Connie

As Marti Lambeth and I interacted further, I asked where exactly in Columbia she lived.

"On Oakland Gravel Road."

"Oakland Gravel Road!? I live on Blue Ridge which intersects with Oakland Gravel Road!"

Further into our conversation, Marti mentioned that the subdivision in which she lived had been developed and purchased from a good friend whose name was Jim Sears.

"Jim Sears!? He lives just three doors to the East of our house!" This, to me, was just another "I'm still here; I will not leave you or forsake you" coincidence orchestrated by God.

From: Connie McClellan
Subject: Today the doctors gave us an estimated departure date from Tampa to Columbia. And...the answer is... the Tuesday before...
Date: Tue, 31 Oct 2006 7:34 PM

THANKSGIVING! Do you believe it?!? I thought for sure the doctor was going to say Christmas. When he said Thanksgiving, I thought I was going to faint! Thank you, Jesus! (AGAIN!)

Once John is home, he will continue rehabilitation on an outpatient basis. We don't know how long the rehabilitation process will be. It's going to take a tremendous amount of effort on John's part, but he's certainly up to the task. After all, he's one of the few, the proud, A MARINE! He won't get the skull cap (where the bullet exited the back of his head) put back into his head for 6 mos, so he'll have to wear that goofy helmet when he's out, but that's okay, he's resolved to it.

By the by, did I mention that his voice is NORMAL!? Goodbye Marlon, hello Johnny Mac! Woo Hoo!

Don't stop praying, as we aren't there yet, but boy are we on our way, thank you, Lord!

Love to All,
Connie

P.S. Also, I heard from my friend, Debbie Leddy, that they had a guest on the 5th floor at Bethesda National Naval Medical Center the other day. YES... very exciting...it was...Billy Joel's brother-in-law! I am so sorry I missed that...ha!... j/k)

One of the things I hated to leave behind in Bethesda was the excitement of the mystery guests; however, it seems that since we left, we haven't missed anything...unless you're a Billy Joel brother-in-law fan...ha!

P.P.S. Debbie said that Dave is doing better. He walked up a flight of stairs today. He's still experiencing the nausea thing, but he's being brave. Please continue to pray for his full recovery and for his pain to go away entirely!

Constantly we received support, prayers and encouragement via e-mail, cards and telephone from family, friends, friends of friends, and even people we didn't know. From the time we learned of John's injury, we received more than 600 cards and letters, half of which were from total strangers. In addition, we received well over 400 e-mails and by the time we arrived in Tampa, my e-mail address book had grown to 350, all people wanting to know first hand about John's progress.

From: gregg morgan
Sent: Tue 10/31/2006 9:54 PM
To: Connie McClellan
Subject: Outstanding Missouri Citizen

Connie, I have been contacted by the honorable Jeff Harris's office regarding nomination for John as an Outstanding Missouri Citizen, for his outstanding service to our country. This would entail being able to be present during the legislative session and recognized on the Missouri House of Representatives floor as well as being presented a proclamation from the Governor. He would need to be available to be present sometime between January and May. Mr. Harris's office (Wanda) would like me to advise.

I mean, it's not the commander in chief, the Secretary of Defense, or Billy Joel's brother-in-law but I think that it is great that John Mac will be honored. What a great way to open the 2007 session. I think we should do this the day the session opens.

So glad to hear of the excellent progress on a daily basis. Please let me know if you need anything at all.
Love,
Gregg

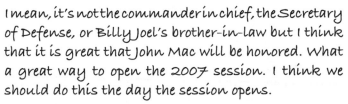

From: Connie McClellan
Sent: Wed 11/1/2006 4:41 AM
To: gregg morgan
Subject: RE: Outstanding Missouri Citizen

Oh Gregg...
Outstanding Missourian?!?!?   How awesome is that?!?... makes me tear up.

The timing is perfect as John will be in Columbia for at least 4 months, as he can't go anywhere until he gets the skull plate reinserted which is no less than six months from the time of the incident. So, that puts him at about the end of March. On behalf of Johnny Mac, I accept the honor (I haven't asked him, but there are some decisions that a mother is allowed to make, and by golly...this is one of them...lol. Actually I'm POSITIVE he would want to accept. Wow...what an honor!)

You are the best!
Love, Connie

From: Connie McClellan
Subject: Today in Tampa...
Date: Wed, 1 Nov 2006 21:27:41-0500

Hi Everyone!
John had an EMG done today to test the facial nerve on his left side. Sadly, it didn't have any activity; however, I AM NOT DISMAYED! In the name of Jesus, that nerve will either regenerate, or the doctors will be able to do the nerve transplant from the nerve in his leg. Either way, it will be taken care of. They tell us they can't do the nerve transplant before 12

136

months, as they need to be sure the nerves aren't going to regenerate on their own.

Please pray:

Lord, if it is your will to heal John immediately, then, go for it. Otherwise, if for whatever reason you choose to wait for the 12 months for the alternatives mentioned above, then so be it. Your ways are higher than ours, Lord. We trust you, and thank you for the patience that you give us in this situation, along with your peace that surpasses all understanding.

Also, Lord, we continue to pray for your angels to protect John's buds in Haditha every minute of every day. Thank you, Lord, that you are SOOOOOOOO faithful, in Jesus' name. Amen.

John walked 300 steps with his walker today! AND...he was able to stand without ANY support for at least 5 seconds. He & I were so excited that he was able to keep his balance while standing. We KNOW that he is going to be able to walk and keep his balance without any problem. This was a VERY encouraging day!

137

Love to all,
Connie

From: Connie McClellan
Date: 11/1/07 6:50 AM
Subject: List of things to be healed.

God is SO good! He just continues to do stuff that blows our minds. He has REALLY strutted His stuff in John's situation. And, he AIN'T THROUGH YET!

At this point, the only things that God is waiting to blow our minds further on are:

1.) restoration of activity in the left side of John's face which will restore his eyebrow, eyelid, and mouth activity on the left side. (I can't wait to see that left dimple again on his cheek).

2.) good vision in the left eye (at this time it is very blurry)

3.) restoration of hearing in the left ear

4.) elimination of ringing in the left ear

5.) restoration of full balance

6.) restoration of full short term memory (his long term memory is great, but, for example, if you give him four words to remember, 30 minutes later he can't remember them all...ha! I think maybe I've got brain trauma, too...LOL)

7.) overall restoration of strength, especially in the left arm and leg

8.) complete elimination of headaches (mostly in the back where the skull plate is missing, but occasionally in the front above his forehead.)

THAT IS ALL! Really and truly, he can live with all of the above and have a full life, but I know that's NOT what God wants for him.

Thank you, Lord, in the name of Jesus that ALL of these things will be restored &/or fixed. Amen.

I love you guys!

Connie

18

November 2, 2006 – November 5, 2006

Two-Three (2/3) Echo's officers continually e-mailed to let us know what was going on back in Haditha. Receiving the e-mails helped us to know how the boys were doing as well as letting us know what progress, if any, was being made in their efforts.

139

From: Atkins 1stSgt Darryl L Sent: Thu 11/2/2006 6:54 AM
To: Connie McClellan
Subject: RE: 2/3 Echo Company
Classification: UNCLASSIFIED

Connie,

Glad to see John is doing so well. I post the majority of the stuff you send and make sure that the Marines know what's going on with him. We are shocked to see that he will be headed home so quickly from such a devastating injury. That is what the power of prayer can do for you.

There seems be some concern about the welfare of the Marines. Here is an update and to keep some of the Moms in the loop. LCpl Carhahan leg was broken in operations yesterday. I talked to him personally before he was medevacked and he was all right and in good spirits. Well, as all right a person can be with a broken leg. LCpl Rankin is at home on convalescent leave.

We have one of the dirtiest and grimiest jobs that you have in one of the most dangerous places in the world. We have had casualties, but we are fighting a determined enemy. We have prepared our Marines as much as possible, but there are some things you can't prepare them for....the devastations you will see in combat. You can give all the classes you want to; you won't know until you see it up close and personal.

140

On a daily basis, I ensure that the platoon commanders, platoon sergeants, squad leaders, and team leaders continuously talk to our Marines about any problems that they might have or think they might have. I believe communication is the key for this, and I'm making sure our Marines communicate. I frown on that "big, bad Marine" concept when it comes to asking for help. If they need help in any way, shape or form, we will ensure that they get it.

The battalion chaplain comes to our position regularly, (we are fortunate, he is near us) and in the next few days, we will have a psychiatrist here to talk to any of our Marines that think that they need to talk. We will ensure that we do everything in our power to help our Marines, your sons.
1stSgt D. L. Atkins

Echo Company
2nd Bn 3rd Marines
Haditha City, Iraq

Reputation is what the world thinks a man is;
character is what he really is.

John continued to make huge strides in his
recovery...

From: Connie McClellan
Subject: 380 steps and counting!
Date: Fri, 3 Nov 2006 06:09:23 -0500

Yesterday, John walked 380 steps in his walker.
The day before was 300; before that 200; before
that 150; before that 80. EVERY day he's gaining
more strength and more balance. Yesterday he
was able to stand without assistance, and without
losing his balance for over 10 seconds. That doesn't
sound like much to us, but trust me...that is
HUUUUUUUUUUGE! We are THRILLED with
the progress. He is truly having to learn to walk
again, but he's doing great.
Also, he has GAINED 10 pounds just in the past week!

141

Please pray:
Lord, in the name of Jesus, we thank You that he
will not need a wheelchair when he comes home on
the 21st of November, and that You will keep him
safe and not allow him to fall.

And, in the meantime, Lord, we thank you that you
continue to watch over his buds in Haditha. We ask
this in the precious name of Jesus, Amen.

We are looking forward to his weekend pass. We're going to Busch Gardens on Sunday. However, the doc says he can't go on the roller coaster. Honestly, doctors are SO paranoid and overprotective sometimes...lol...oh well, I guess we'll do what they say...ha!

Love to all!
Connie

P.S. Go to 'http://www.stripes.com/article.asp?section=104&article=40260&archive=true' to view today's Stars & Stripes online publication. They have written the "sequel" to last October's story about John. At the bottom, there's a link to last October's article for those of you who may have missed it.

142

More bad news from Haditha...

From: David Kelm Sent: Sat 11/4/2006 8:01 PM
To: Connie McClellan
Subject: Re: More information on John's platoon

Hi, Mrs. McClellan,

Sorry I don't get to write very often, but it's great when I do get to sit down and read everything about John. Unfortunately one of our Marines was killed in that incident you referenced. His name is Daniel Chaires from Tallahassee, FL. He was one of ours from First Platoon. His loss was and still is tough to bear, but it was not in vain. As I'm sure you hear, we continue to take the fight to the enemy and see results. Attacks have dropped off dramatically (and the weather is a lot more comfortable). Please tell John that I continue to keep him and all of you in my prayers. As always, God bless.

Yours,
Dave Kelm

From: Connie McClellan
Subject: FW: Please pray for Daniel Chaires
Date: Sun, 5 Nov 2006 08:03 AM

Please pray:
Thank you, Lord, in the name of Jesus that you are reaching down and touching Daniel's family in a mighty way, showing them You are real, giving them Your peace that surpasses all understanding, letting them know that this is not the end all, and that they will see Daniel again...in heaven. Amen.

143

From: Connie McClellan
Subject: E-mail from Dave Kelm (John's Company Lieutenant)
Date: Sun, 5 Nov 2006 06:30 AM

Please pray for the families of all the Marines referenced in the following e-mail from Dave Kelm.

Lt. David Kelm
Sent: Sat 11/4/2006 8:49 PM
Subject: Marhabtien

Hello All,

Arabic, of course, for two hellos, marhabtien expresses sincere respect and friendship for the person to whom you extend the greeting.

Things here have calmed down a lot. Ramadan was no joke, they really turned it up a few notches. We would see as many as nine different attacks in one day, now we see about 2-3 per day. It was pretty ugly, we've lost six so far here in our city, four from Echo. One of them was mine, Daniel Chaires, from Tallahassee, FL. Please keep him and his parents in your prayers. He was probably the most loyal person I've ever met, and I don't think I'll ever meet a person as genuinely good as him. We all miss him very much. As far as my platoon goes, we've been fairly fortunate. With the exception of John and Daniel, everything has been minor gunshot wounds or fragmentation wounds; nobody else has gone home. BUT MAKE NO MISTAKE, ECHO COMPANY IS KICKING ASS... Period. We've confirmed killed 3-4 times more insurgents than they get of us, heard reports of wounding a bunch more, and these guys are straight up scared to attack us. The Iraqi Police will be here soon, en masse, and their leader has a plan to turn this place around. Spirits are very high around here because we can see the progress being made every week.

THANK YOU to everyone sending packages for me and my Marines. Lately I have been overwhelmed by your well-wishes and generosity, to include weekly cards from my favorite war protestor and huge packages from people that I used to make cry. Anyway, please keep them coming as much as you care to, the Marines really need to know that people are thinking of them.

So that's the party line, besides that everyone's fine.

144

We get pretty run down at times, but we always get a day where we can catch our breath for a while. Just hearing from home is pretty much the highlight of everyone's time here. Having said that, because you all seem so bent on requests of what to send, here are some things you can send the guys if you want to for Christmas or something:

-Cigarettes - send as many as you care to, these guys never stop, it's disgusting
-Alarm clocks
-Flashlights
-Coffee/coffee makers
-Tupperware bowls
-Twin sheets
-Protein powder
-Mac & Cheese
-Campbell's chunky soup (big crowd pleaser)
-Mechanical pencils and pens
-And, of course, candy for our Iraqi friends

145

Anyway, gotta go again. As always, hope this finds you well.

Dave

From: Connie McClellan
Date: Mon, 6 Nov 2006 07:18 AM
Subject: John walked 600 feet!

Good morning, everyone!
Yesterday John walked with his walker all around the interior perimeter of the hotel. Carl measured it, - over 600 feet. John walked that track two times in one afternoon! AND, he didn't need to take a nap, which means his endurance is improving.

John and I were talking about how we take the performance of our bodies SOOOOOOO for granted. He is literally, having to learn to walk again. It is very frustrating, as you can imagine; however, he is determined. His balance is still causing problems. He made the comment yesterday that he hoped he'll be able to walk again. I assured him that he would, but it was going to take a lot of hard work and perseverance on his part.

Please pray:

Thank you, Lord, in the name of Jesus, that John's balance and walking ability will be completely restored, along with any other deficiencies, and that he will not have to have a wheelchair when we return to Columbia. Also, Lord, take away any doubt that he has that this will happen, give him the assurance and peace that he needing at this time, Amen.
Love to all,
Connie

146

John felt frustration in many areas, but learning to walk again proved to be his biggest challenge. One day after we'd been in Tampa for about a week, we were working with John's physical therapist, Juan José Vallada. In desperation John vowed, "Juan José, before I leave here if you can get me to where I can walk, I'll give you one of my purple hearts."

I blurted, "John! No, No! You can't do that!"

He argued, "Mom, I'm serious, I'll give him a purple heart if he can get me to walk."

"John...you *can't* do that!"

At that point, Juan piped in, "No, John...really...you can't do that."

Fortunately, Juan didn't hold him to it, as before long, John *was* walking. However, it served as another example of why it's important for parents to be with their Marines during recovery, or they'd come home without *any medals at all!*

147

19

November 8, 2006 – November 13, 2006

As time progressed, my Tampa e-mail updates became less frequent and dramatic, but it didn't mean there wasn't a tremendous amount of activity on our end. Each day consisted of one therapy after another: Occupational, Speech, Physical, Recreational and Psychological. In between, there were desperately needed times of rest as well as various events going on at the hospital. Often there were special lunches or gatherings, sponsored by different organizations, and these helped to break the monotony of the days' routines.

From: Connie McClellan
Subject: Another GREAT day in Tampa!
Date: Wed, 8 Nov 2006 06:30 AM

Yesterday, John walked 400 steps without a walker with only his physical therapist using a chest strap to help him keep his balance. This was the first day

John has been really encouraged that he really will someday walk again, so needless to say he was VERY pleased.

Yesterday morning the Marines had a cake cutting ceremony for the 231st birthday of the Marine Corps. They let the youngest Marine and the oldest Marine at the hospital be the recipients of the first pieces of cake. John was the youngest and an 80 year old veteran was the oldest. They had some of the Marine big wigs to conduct the ceremony. It was very cool.

Then, five of the Tampa Bay Buccaneers came by for a photo shoot...very, very cool.
Love to all, Connie

From: Connie McClellan
Date: 11/9/06 5:50 Am
Subject: Update from Tampa

149

Yesterday, John did even better with walking in Physical Therapy. More and more he's feeling more in control of the balance thing. He, and we, are all encouraged by his progress.

Also, yesterday was the first time that John wanted to talk on the phone. (Any other time, I've had to practically beg him to make calls, as he just didn't feel like it). Carl & I went back to the hotel around 5:00 and then to get some decent food to bring back (yesterday's dinner at the hospital was pretty bad, so John specifically requested stuffed steak burritos from Taco Bell...lol). Anyway, by the time we got back, my cell phone that I had left with him was totally out of juice because he'd been calling and talking ever since we left. I was elated!

Tomorrow night we're all going to the Marine Ball (Carl is going, too!) It's going to be quite the affair. The Marines have rented John a Tuxedo. John has a 3-day pass which will be great. Then, Jane comes in on Saturday, so we're going to have quite the reunion!

Love to all!

Connie

From: Connie McClellan
Date: 11/10/06 9:10 M
Subject: Update on Therapy

150

Yesterday, John had a pretty routine day EXCEPT for the Recreational Therapy. They took him to Blockbuster to get a movie. This is not normally a big deal, except it was for John as he walked (with the chest strap and his Physical Therapist holding with one hand to keep him balanced in case he started to sway) from the second floor all the way down to the vehicle, all around Blockbuster, and all the way back from the vehicle to his floor including two flights of stairs. The distance from his room to the vehicle is no less than 1000 feet. Needless to say, he was VERY tired!

Then, tomorrow we'll pick up Jane at the airport and head to the beach where we will stay in the condo donated for our use by St. Charles Farmers Agent, Mark Arnold. THANK YOU, MARK! Jane's birthday is on Monday, so we'll be celebrating this weekend....BIG TIME!. What a great thing to have her here for her birthday. She said it's the best birthday present she could have. John has come so far since she left us in Bethesda after that first week, I can't wait to get her reaction.

Please continue to pray for John's buds in Haditha: Thank you, Lord, that you are protecting all of John's buds, keeping your angels watching over them every minute of every day, in Jesus' name. Amen.

By the by...John said yesterday that he doesn't have headache pain anymore...THANK YOU, LORD! Woo Hoo!
Love to All!

Connie

We continued to hear from the brave parents of John's friends in Iraq. Knowing how they worried about their own sons, I never ceased to be touched by their affection and concern for John.

151

From: Carl & Rhonda Smith
Sent: Fri 11/10/2006 1:04 PM
To: Connie McClellan;
Subject: Phone Call from Trent Smith to his Mom & Dad

Trent called this morning. The connection was amazingly good, but we still were cut off 4 times. He said he was doing well. Although they aren't as busy as during Ramadan, they are still very busy. He mentioned that it seems like they are getting mail a little quicker.

He said they got to see the Stars & Stripes article about Johnny Mac. They are happy he is doing so well.

Trent saw Chuck Norris when he was there. He didn't think Norris was coming to the base, just the dam. When Trent went to the chow hall to get a Gatorade, he saw a bunch of food all laid out. "I wondered what was going on 'cause they would never have something like that out for us. Then one of the guys I was with said, 'Hey look, Chuck Norris!' I couldn't see him 'cause he was sitting down and had on a camo shirt and hat to blend in. Then I spotted him, he had a fanny pack. I thought that was funny.'

152

Trent also told us the Chaplain comes around about once a week or more and that there is a counselor if they need to talk to someone. He said morale is high and they are doing well.

Smitty's Dad

From: Connie McClellan
Date: 11/11/06 6:10 AM
Subject: Did we have a ball at the ball?

Lol...not really...but I wouldn't have missed it for anything. And the only reason we didn't have a REALLY good time is that there were over 1000 people there, NONE of whom we knew. BUT other than that, it was wonderful seeing all of the men in their fully dressed uniforms and the women.... oh my gosh...wearing every formal gown known to man....lol...or should I say, Wo-man...ha! It was really something.

As I've explained, the nerve in the left side of his face affects his left eyebrow, eyelid and left side of his mouth. It has much the same effect as someone who's had a stroke. As a result, he is not able to fully smile (smile is very one-sided, which is why he won't do it for the camera. Also, his left eye is puffy because of the gold weight that was put in it to keep closed. BUT DO REMEMBER, mentally, he is the same, even though he looks different. BUT...John's "joy" has not yet been restored. I guess if we would all put ourselves in his shoes, with the disabilities that he is enduring (i.e. balance problems, walking challenges, paralyzed left face, TOTAL dependence on other people), we probably wouldn't have our joy either. However, they tell me with a brain injury that it is not uncommon for one day... POOF...that the joy will be restored.

153

JOHN, CARL & CONNIE AT THE MARINE BALL

Please pray: Thank you, Lord, in the name of Jesus that John's joy is restored...SOON. Amen

Connie

Throughout John's recovery experience, people consistently extended us their generosity. As an example, John's Uncle Jim and cousin, Jamie, drove six hours from Jacksonville, Florida to treat us to a Steak 'n Shake lunch and an elegant Stonewood Restaurant dinner. In addition, they went shopping and bought John a whole new wardrobe of Under Armour® garb which he wore every day from then on.

Then, Mark Arnold, a business acquaintance of Carl's, donated his Clearwater Beach condo for us to use as long as we desired. Normally, he rented it out this time of year, but when he heard we were going to be in the area, he took it off the market. We thoroughly enjoyed and appreciated his incredible act of kindness and generosity.

From: Connie McClellan
Date: 11/13/06 5:50 AM
Subject: A beautiful Weekend at the beach

Good morning!

Saturday we left Tampa to pick up Jane at the airport. From there we went to Clearwater and stayed at a FABULOUS condo donated by our St. Charles friend, Mark Arnold. It was so beautiful...our front yard was the ocean except for the swimming pool and club house in between. WOW!

Then back to the hospital last night for the 8:00 PM bell. John was very tired as he hadn't taken a nap all day and he did a lot of walking. (No walker, only with a chest strap for us to "spot" him with, but he hardly needed our help.) The balance thing is still an issue, but less and less all the time.

This morning he's in Rec Therapy Arts and Crafts... ha...anyone who knows John knows how much he's enjoying that! Poor guy...

Anyway, today will be pretty routine EXCEPT... this afternoon at 3:00 they're taking his feeding tube out. This is VERY exciting!

Love, Connie

155

20

November 14, 2006 –
November 19, 2006

156

Finally, the day had come for the doctors to remove John's feeding tube. Good news: He wouldn't have that "tail" hanging down between his legs. Bad news: I couldn't poke fun at him anymore. You can be sure, for John, the prospect of not having the "tube teasing" was a pleasant one. For some medical reason, the doctors had to wait no less than 30 days from the time the tube was inserted to remove it, even though John hadn't needed it for the last two weeks. Having that tube removed served as a milestone for John as it represented the last foreign appendage attached to his body. He had come such a long way with the removal of the brain shunt, breathing tube, the nose tube, the IV tubes...and now... the feeding tube...certainly cause for rejoicing.

From: Connie McClellan
Sent: Tuesday, November 14, 2006 5:37 AM
Subject: They pulled the plug!

The feeding tube peg plug that is. It went fine. John is now plug-free! He has NO MORE foreign appendages coming out of his body. Have we come a long way or WHAT!? Thank you, Lord!

Yesterday, John walked with a cane during physical therapy. He had on the "safety chest strap allowing Juan to "spot" him, but no action was necessary on Juan's part. . It is so amazing the progress John has made just in the 3 weeks he has been in Tampa. To think, he had hardly been in a wheelchair before he got on the C-130 gurney journey from Bethesda to Tampa....wow...truly awesome.

Love to all.

Connie

From: Connie McClellan
Date: 11/15/06 6:20 AM
Subject: Another Great Day in Tampa

157

Yesterday was another great day! The majority of John's Physical Therapy was walking with a cane. Then, his physical therapist had him do side walking using what I call the "Hava Nagila" steps, you know where one foot goes behind the other and so on down the hall. I was VERY pleased with how well he did that move! I told him he can "line dance" with the best of them! (We both laughed as we both know he HATES dancing....lol)
Another wonderful occurrence that I forgot to mention: Day before yesterday John went to group therapy (which we all know he LOVES....ha!). As always, he left his room grumbling on the way to group therapy, but since it's not optional, he had no choice. ANYWAY, I guess when he was there,

he met a new guy who is close to his age. They started the laughing thing (you know where you start laughing for no memorable reason and then can't stop, and then when you do, you look at the other person and start all over again?). I guess they had a BIG time. THEN, when John came back to his room, he started chuckling. He explained what had happened. I asked what started it. He said he didn't have a clue and then........he BURST out laughing. I thought the right side of smile was going to jump off his face, it was so big. Of course, it was a VERY one-sided smile, but it was FABULOUS!- Then, it became contagious with all of us. We all (Carl, Jane, John & I) HOWLED! This was SO HUGE as THIS is the joy restoration that we've been praying and looking for. Thank you, LORD!

158

Today, we go for the eye exam. Please pray: Thank you, Lord, in the name of Jesus, that the sight in John's left eye can be restored, one way or the other. Amen

I told John, glasses are very vogue right now, so if that's how God chooses to clear up that left eye, then that is fine with us, but, of course, if God chooses to miraculously restore the sight naturally, we are VERY good with that. (If that happens and John is disappointed that he won't be vogue with the glasses thing, I told him we can always get him a pair of glasses with lenses that just have clear glass in them...lol).

Love to all!

Connie

From: Connie McClellan
Date: 11/15/06 8:50 PM
Subject: If there is a Guinness Book of
World Record for the person who has received
the most miracles...

I'm pretty sure John Mac has just broken it! Listen to this:

We went for the eye exam. His right eye is 20/20. His left eye's optic nerve and retina are in perfect shape. His cornea is "rough," but the doctor tells us that should heal itself. Once the eyelid closes, we won't have to use the ointment every 4 hours which, of course, makes his vision blurry. Once the cornea repairs itself AND we don't have the ointment induced blurriness, the doctor said he sees no reason why John's vision will not return to 20/20 in the left eye! DO YOU BELIEVE IT?! Thank you, Lord!

ANOTHER GREAT DAY IN TAMPA, FL!

Love to all!

Connie

159

When I received the eye report, I couldn't help but reflect on the initial September '06 prognosis and the fear that John might be totally blind, and how at the time, we were   actually resolved to that possibility. Praise the Lord, we didn't have to "do blind."

Every day I received at least one e-mail from a parent of one of John's comrades in Iraq. Mary Jo Gray is the mother of James Steuter, one of John's best friends who was also with him in Afghanistan. The following e-mail was the first I had received from Mary Jo, so I wasn't exactly sure who she was…

From: Gray, Mary Jo
Sent: Friday, November 17, 2006 6:16 AM
Subject: Prayer Request

All,
Please pass this on. James called yesterday. He's doing okay but needs all of our prayers more than ever. They lost three more guys in an IED explosion on his birthday, 11/14, one who was from Lincoln, NE, and this Marine had not yet seen his baby daughter born in Sept. I worry about James every minute of every day and wish for the days to pass quickly until he is home. He's still working 20 + hours a day. He had just taken his first hot shower yesterday at the dam. His normal shower, which he gets every 10 days is from a hose with cold water. Iraq and all he is seeing and doing is really taking a toll on him. Please pray for God's protection and continued blessings to give James strength to get through this.

Thanks to everyone for your continued support.
Love,
MJ

From: Connie McClellan
Sent: Friday, November 17, 2006 8:31 AM
To: Gray, Mary Jo
Subject: RE: Prayer Request

Mary Jo, James is James Steuter? Who were the others killed by the IED?

160

I'm ready to send out to my e-mail entourage, but want to be sure my facts are right.

Thank you, Lord, in the name of Jesus that you are protecting James and his buds, CONSTANTLY, and in the meantime, you give their families the peace that can only come from You. Amen.

From: Gray, Mary Jo
Sent: Fri 11/17/2006 8:37 AM
To: Connie McClellan
Subject: RE: Prayer Request

Yes, James Steuter ~ I'm James' mom. I don't think we've e-mailed each other yet, but have received several e-mails from Trina and Brittany (James's girlfriend) keeping us in the loop of how John is doing and the amazing recovery he is having.

I don't know the names of the other two killed other than they were in the 4th humvee in James's group. The 3rd Marine was Scholl from Lincoln, NE.

Thinking of John, you, and all your family. Our prayers are with you all!
Thanks for your support!
Kind Regards,
Mary Jo

The same day I received the e-mail from Mary Jo, I received another e-mail from Dave Kelm clarifying that he and some of his Marines were with the patrol on which the IED detonated. Fortunately, none of his 2/3 Echo Marines were hurt; however, that incident did result in the death of three Marines and one who sustained severe injuries. In his e-mail he relayed, "I can't say/don't want to say anything more about it other than it was a pretty crappy day all around. Other than the tragic deaths and injury, things have been going well here. The Iraqi policemen have finally arrived, and are in force. There are over 100 of them here. A few of us took them out on their first big patrol tonight,; they're surprisingly competent. We said goodbye to our Iraqi Army soldiers though, as they've headed across the river to another town. They kept quitting because obviously things aren't so fun around here sometimes, so their battalion sent them to a different area."

E-mails such as these provided pertinent information about what was really going on with the war, always a huge contrast from what we heard on the news.

21

November 20, 2006 – November 21, 2006

The time was rapidly approaching for our trip home on November 21st; however, in the meantime John's therapy continued along with other events...

From: Connie McClellan
Date: Mon, 20 Nov 2006 06:32:35 -0500
Subject: John honored at Tampa Bay Buccaneers' Half-time

163

Yesterday was a great day for John. We went to the Tampa Bay Buccaneer/ Washington Redskins game. John and another wounded soldier got to sit in the glassed in box with General and Mrs. Diamond. They viewed the game in a VERY nice, air-conditioned box with VERY good food.

It was Armed Forces Day at the game, so during halftime 122 new recruits from all 4 branches of the services were inducted. John and Lee Jones (wounded Army soldier) were on the field and honored by the 50000+ people there. The stadium was full They rolled John & Lee in their wheelchairs around the perimeter of the field and people were cheering and thanking them all the way around. It was very moving. AND, it was a great game...AND the Bucs won!

After the game, John and Lee were escorted to the locker room to meet the Bucs. Each player signed a football for both John and Lee. THEN...Coach Gruden literally gave John the shirt off his back. John is going to wear it on the plane home on Tuesday. It goes really well with his Marine sweat pants. Another player gave him his glove. They also got to meet the Buc's cheerleaders. You can be sure that was a highlight.

Tomorrow...we are...OUTTA HERE! Halleluiah!

Love to all,
Connie

P.S. Thank you, Lord, in the name of Jesus for protecting John's buds back in Haditha, so they can come home whole in every way, physically, emotionally, mentally, and spiritually, and, in the meantime, give their families the peace that surpasses ALL understanding. Amen

I found the Tampa Bay fans to be amazingly loyal. When we attended that game, their record for the season was 2-6, yet the game sold out. In fact, the Marines had to pull some strings just to get me a ticket in the cheap seats.

We learned that Tampa Bay's Coach Gruden had an amazing resemblance to Chuckie, the evil doll in the

Chuckie movies. Here in Missouri, everyone drives around with Tiger tails hanging off of their bumpers, but in Tampa, the fans drove around with Chuckie dolls hanging out of their sunroofs! I really admired Coach Gruden as he seemed to take it all in stride. What a good sport he was!

That evening the Marines delivered us back to the hospital circle drive, where we were greeted by several military "brass" who introduced themselves and then presented John with his last two coins. I felt this was symbolic of the culmination of our two month, away-from-home experience since John's injury.

On the morning of Tuesday, November 21ˢᵗ, as John and I packed his things, we checked the closets and drawers one more time to be sure we hadn't missed anything. After placing the last shirt in, I zipped the suitcase and stood facing John for a moment I will never forget. With tears welling in my eyes, I gave him a fierce hug and expressed, "John, it's been an honor and a privilege being with you these last two months."

Tenderly, he responded, "Oh Mom, I don't know what I would have done without you." It still makes me tear up just thinking about it.

22

November 21, 2006 – December 2, 2006

From the moment we left the hospital for the airport, we were treated as royalty. When we arrived at Tampa International Airport, several people greeted us as our vehicle pulled to the curb. Leading this welcoming committee was the head of the Transportation Security Administration for Tampa International and he proved invaluable, allowing us to sidestep the majority of the security checks.

Immediately, another of those that greeted us began working on upgrading our tickets to First Class. Neither John nor I had ever before flown First Class, so we were elated when they announced their upgrading efforts had been successful for the flight to Chicago. What a trip! In my opinion, the Chicago flight even surpassed the C130 flight to Tampa. In John's opinion, there was no contest between First Class and the C130.

The best part came immediately after the plane landed in Chicago and connected to the passenger ramp. The overhead lights turned on and the seatbelt signs turned off, which was our queue to stand and prepare to deplane. As John grabbed his cane and I gathered our carry-on bags, the captain's voice came over the loud speaker. "Ladies and Gentlemen, I want to let you know we are honored to have Marine LCpl. John McClellan on board with us this morning. LCpl. McClellan is returning home for the first time since being severely injured in Iraq. We welcome those of you who would like, to show your appreciation to LCpl. McClellan." As John and I headed for the exit, everyone started clapping and cheering. As long as I live, I will never forget the emotions of that moment.

We retrieved John's wheelchair and I rolled him to the gate for our next flight from Chicago to St. Louis. We suspected and hoped we might again be bumped to First Class, but wouldn't know for sure until we boarded. As John and I walked onto the plane we compared the aisle number on our boarding passes to the number above the seats. When each of us realized we had indeed, again, been bumped to First Class, we looked at each other and immediately implemented a "high five." John told me he's going to take his wheelchair, helmet and Marine shirt on ALL of his future flights. I'm *pretty* sure he was just kidding.

We landed in St. Louis and, again, as we prepared to deplane, the captain came over the intercom and, again, introduced John, exactly as had been done on the previous flight. I've often wondered who was responsible for informing the pilots.

Throughout both airports, people continually walked up and thanked John for his service, but the *real* highlight occurred when we landed in Columbia. John and I were in the very front seat of the commuter plane, so we didn't have any windows, but as the plane was pulling into the terminal, we could hear the other passengers talking about all the commotion outside, wondering aloud, "What the heck is going on?" A huge crowd of people, all with American flags, stood on the other side of the fence awaiting our arrival. The pilot instructed us to let the other passengers deplane first. A couple of times, the crowd apparently thought they saw John coming out, so they started cheering and then stopped when they realized it wasn't him. This occurred one more time when they thought it was John coming out. *Finally*, when John stuck his head out of the plane, a resounding cheer came up from the crowd. This time the cheering did not stop until we entered the terminal. What an amazing welcome we had!

The icing on the cake came with the Columbia Police escort from the airport to our home, where we reunited with family and friends. Thanksgiving, 2006, had a whole new meaning for the McClellan family!

Meanwhile, back in Iraq...

COLUMBIA HOMECOMING, NOVEMBER 21, 2006

169

JOHN WITH COLUMBIA POLICE DEPARTMENT MOTORCYCLE
ESCORT, NOVEMBER 21, 2006.

From: Atkins 1stSgt Darryl L
Sent: Thu 11/23/2006 12:12 AM
To: Connie McClellan
Subject: RE: 2/3 Echo Company

Connie,

Glad to see that things are coming along well for John. Tell him everybody here is doing well. Things here are the same. It's gotten colder over the last couple of days. Let him know that Sgt Davidson reenlisted. It surprised everybody here. A couple of days ago, he was asking advice about what to do when he got out then he reenlisted out of the blue. He's turning out to be a great Marine. On a bad note, we had three Marines killed by an IED and let him know that SSgt Wilson was devastatingly injured but he's alive. He is at Bethesda hospital now. He lost a leg, the other leg was broken, left arm broken, several broken ribs and very bad lacerations on his face. The doctors are amazed with his constitution. He should be dead but it seems like God has other plans for him. I talked to him a couple of days ago and he's asking me what he can do to help the company. That is what the Marine Corps is about. I don't think people really understand the bond that combat forms with us.

1stSgt D. L. Atkins
Echo Company 2/3
Haditha City, Iraq

Lead me, follow me, or get out of my way. - George S. Patton

170

Immediately following Thanksgiving vacation, John began a daily regimen of Physical, Occupational and Speech Therapy at Rusk Rehabilitation Center, located less than two miles from our home. He attended for two and one-quarter hours in the mornings and in the afternoons he took advantage of Xbox 360 (video game) therapy!

This actually worked pretty well to help his left hand regain its movement. Carl and I returned to our jobs as insurance agents. Finally, our lives were beginning to return to normal.

My e-mails continued, but with the redundancy of John's routine, they were not nearly as frequent or newsworthy...

From: Connie McClellan
Date: 11/29/06
Subject: John's therapy is going well

I've had many people call to ask how John's doing at Rusk. He is doing great! He is doing Physical Therapy, Speech Therapy and Occupational Therapy. And, in the afternoons, he get visits from all of his friends who play XBox with him and help his left hand recover at the same time. It's been great having all of his friends over again!

You can't believe how much he has improved starting immediately after he got home. He doesn't use a cane at all in the house. He's still got a ways to go, though, so don't stop praying for him until I tell you............lol. In the meantime, please pray:

171

Thank you, Lord, that you are healing John's 1.) Imbalance which affects his ability to walk well 2.) left ear hearing 3.) left side of face and 4.) short-term memory. And, also, Lord, we continue to pray for the protection of all of John's buds back in Haditha. All of these we pray in Jesus' name. Amen.

Do you believe it is down to these four things?! God is SOOOOOOOOOO good!

Did I tell you how wonderful our Thanksgiving was. If I didn't, it was SOOOOOOOO wonderful!! If I did, sorry for the redundancy.........lol

Love to all!

Connie

172

Debbie Leddy and I continued to keep in contact regularly. I received this fascinating e-mail from her, after which I googled as she suggested. The enemy are such liars!

From: Debbie Leddy
DATE: 11/30/07
Subject: Info from Debbie Leddy as to how insurgents got Dave's billfold.

Connie

Google David Leddy Marine and on the page that comes up first look at the 2nd thing listed Jawa report. Click on that and then read it and scroll down and you will see Dave's picture. Apparently, the Marines who found Dave, cut off his pants and when they did this they cut off his wallet with the ID card. The bad guys found his wallet and posted his picture on a website, saying that he was dead. What liars they are.

173

23

December 3, 2006 - December 26, 2006

Initially, while living at home with us, John had a steady stream of friends and family stopping in to see him. But the time came when the stream turned to a trickle, as everyone began to go on with their lives.

174

From: Connie McClellan
Date: December 3, 2006   5:58 AM
Subject: Update on John

For those of you in Columbia, stop by and see John sometime. Sadly, the revolving door has come to a halt.

As most of you know, we had a BIG (16") snow here on Friday. It SO reminded me of when John was in school, as whenever there was a chance of school being called off because of bad weather, he would get so excited. Nothing has changed. Thursday night he said he'd hoped it would snow, so he wouldn't have to go to therapy.....Ha....just like old times! He got his wish....Big time!

Everyday that goes by, he's doing better with his

walking. He can go up and down the stairs without any trouble. In fact, he's doing SO well that Carl and I get our bedroom back today...woohoo! lol

Please pray: And, thank you, Lord, for the protection that you giving John's buds back in Haditha, every minute of every day, in your name we pray. Amen.

Love to all,
Connie

When John closed his left eye, there was a gap of about 1/8 inch. Consequently, it was imperative that he keep the eye lubricated with a Vaseline type ointment, in order to prevent the cornea from drying out. This of course, left him with extremely blurry vision...

175

From: Connie McClellan
Date: December 6, 2006 6:08 AM
Subject: Update on John

Good morning!

I wanted to give you an update on John. John is walking better and better everyday. He does not use a cane at all around the house. He goes to therapy (physical, speech and occupational) in the mornings and is home in the afternoons. He is ALWAYS up for visitors, so for those of you in the vicinity, give him a call and stop on by.
One of the things they do in occupational therapy is to work with patients to make them self-sufficient which includes teaching them to cook. Of course, I

was thrilled that is one of the goals, as Carl & I have tried for years to get him to cook...sadly he STILL doesn't like it...lol....poor guy....lol.

Please pray: Thank you for protecting ALL of John's buds in Haditha every minute of every day, bringing them home whole in every way, in Jesus' name we pray. Amen.

Love to all,
Connie

We continued to receive news about our boys in Haditha, and too often it was not good news...

From: Rhonda Smith
Date: December 6, 2006 8:10 AM
Subject: E-mail from Trent Smith's Mom & Dad – Bad news from Haditha

Thanks for the update Connie, and thank you for praying for John's buds. Unfortunately, more sad news for two more Marines from 2/3 that died in the lake by Haditha Dam when they had to jump out of the helicopter. I don't know for sure what company they were from yet but they did release the names. Their names are Major Joseph McCloud and Cpl. Joshua Sticklen. Sorry to be the bearer of bad news. I was just on the Any Soldier Inc. website reading letters from different Marines. It is pretty interesting to go on. John might even know some of the guys on there. It is a web site that you can go and pick out a Marine or other soldier and send care packages to, then they distribute them to other Marines. Carl and I have been sending packages to

Lt. Robert Nelson, he's a Chaplain with 2/3. He just posted a new letter, it's really interesting to read. He was away for a while and came back and there were 70 care packages sent to him! Because he is the Chaplain he knows who is not getting much, so he's great to send things to. Well take care and check out the above website, there are pictures also.

Please send us good news about John!
Take care, Rhonda

From: Connie McClellan
Date: December 6, 2006 08:56 PM
Subject: Results of John's eye appointment.

Okay...well...John had an eye appointment today. I was hoping they could put a little more weight in his eyelid to make his eye close, but the doctors here say to put additional weight on John's eyelid would be so much that he couldn't open his eye, so that's not going to work. So, we'll need to keep the lubrication going until a.) God miraculously heals him b.) the nerves gradually regenerate on their own 3.) the docs do the nerve graft.

177

As I've said before, when we don't get an immediate response to our prayers, it means that a.) what we are praying is not God's will or b.) he has a better plan in the works. I know it is God's will that John be healed, so apparently He's got something better planned. God has proven throughout this experience that He will not leave us or forsake us, so I know He's not about to start now...hmmm...I don't remember praying for patience...lol (You know what they say...Don't ever pray for patience...or God will give you something to be patient about...ha!)

PATIENCE, PATIENCE, PATIENCE...aghhh!

Love to all!
Connie

All of my e-mails went to John's superiors in Iraq, so often I would receive clarification on information I had forwarded...

From: Darryl Atkins
Date: December 6, 2006 08:07:00
Subject: Bad News on 2/3 Echo

178

Connie,

Glad to see that John is doing so well. Things here have slowed down tremendously. The Marines that died were from H & S Company, not Echo.

1stSgt D. L. Atkins
Echo Company 2/3
Haditha City, Iraq

Lead me, follow me, or get out of my way. - George S. Patton:
From: Connie McClellan
Date: December 7, 2006 06:08:00
Subject: E-mail from John's 1ˢᵗ Sgt In Haditha

I am relieved by the above note from 1st Sgt. Darrell Atkins, from John's platoon, however I am still saddened that 3 Marines were killed. Please pray:

Thank you, Lord, that you are with the families and friends of these 3 boys killed in Iraq. Let them know, Lord, that their grief is only temporary and that they will see them again some day in heaven. And for those boys left behind with the memories of these boys' deaths, heal them, Lord, from any Post Traumatic Stress that they may be having or could have. Protect our boys, Lord, protect our boys, in Jesus' name. Amen.

Love to all,
Connie

From: Connie McClellan
Date: December 16, 2006   6:10 AM
Subject: Update in Presidential Prayer Team Newsletter & Update on John

Hi Everyone!

179

I haven't sent out an update lately as the progress John is making is not as newsworthy as what we were experiencing the first two months. HOWEVER....do not misunderstand....he is making progress every day! In fact, last night Carl called to me, "Did you see that?" I asked, "See what?" "John just walked up the stairs without using the railing!"
Actually, it was a good news, bad news thing. The good news was that he was walking up the stairs without using the railing; the bad news was...HE WAS WALKING UP THE STAIRS WITHOUT USING THE RAILING!...THAT IS SO UNSAFE! lol   Oh well....I know God is STILL protecting him, so I'm not going to wig out about it.

Anyway....like I said, he is making progress every day, but we still have the issues of: 1.) balance 2.) left side of face 3.) hearing in left ear, 4.) Short term memory loss, Like I said before, DON'T STOP PRAYING FOR HIM UNTIL I TELL YOU!

Thank you, Lord, that you are healing all of the above in John AND, that you are continuing to protect ALL of John's buds back in Haditha, and in the meantime, you are giving their families the peace that can only come from you, in Jesus' name. Amen.

Love to all,

Connie

180

24

December 27, 2006 - January 13, 2007

The holidays were especially meaningful this year, as we had so much for which we were thankful. Just being together as a family was reward enough, but God had even more in store for us. Right before our eyes we saw God's miracle working power manifested in John's body.

181

From: Connie McClellan
Date: December 27, 2006 5:50 AM
Subject: ANOTHER MIRACLE! You are NOT going to believe this!

Okay...see the attached picture of John and his Tampa speech therapist...take a good look. Then, compare it to the picture "John's new face." The left side of his face is so much better!

Monday, John went to the Lake of the Ozarks with his cousins, Lance & Larry Loethen. Apparently, they were laughing the entire time, which must be the best therapy, because...when he got home we noticed right away that the left side of his mouth is turned up AND his eye is closing almost all the way. AND, he discovered when he smiles, he can see the top of his cheek lift up! THIS IS SO HUGE! This is progress that was not anticipated by his doctors. AND, it's only be one month since we got home. UNBELIEVABLE!

No...MIRACULOUS! Thank you, Jesus...AGAIN! or should I say STILL since He's been working with John without stopping. It's just that we're just now able to see it. But obviously, there is amazing, miraculous growth going on behind those cheeks!

Anyway, I just wanted you to share in our joy!

As you might expect, we had a WONDERFUL Christmas and it had nothing to do with the presents, but EVERYTHING to do with John's presence!

Love to all, Connie

When John returned home from the weekend with Lance and Larry, he and his best friend, Allen, were on our deck, laughing and carrying on, when John asked Allen, "Dude! Can you see my left cheek lift up when I smile?"

Allen watched John smile/frown/smile/frown and blurted, "Yes! I do! It *is* lifting up!"

That revelation was the first sign that, after only four months, the left side of John's face had begun to restore. What a great day that turned out to be for the McClellan Family!

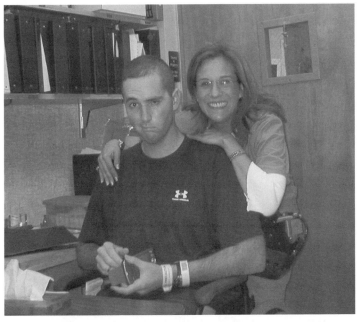

John with Speech Therapist, Linda Picon, at Tampa V.A. 11/21/06

183

"John's New Face" This picture was taken the day we realized John smile had expanded and his cheek lifted up. 12/27/06

After we returned to Columbia, John's days were amazingly busy as he had Physical, Occupational and Speech Therapy at Rusk Rehabilitation in the morning and a continual string of Neurology, Audiology, and Ophthalmology appointments on many of the afternoons.

One of the earlier appointments attended was Audiology. After extensive testing on his left ear, we learned his left ear had no activity. This meant John would not be a hearing aid candidate. However, the doctors introduced us to a fascinating device called a BAHA (Bone Anchored Hearing Accessory) that might help John's left ear. A screw would be surgically inserted into the left side of his skull, then after several months of healing, the BAHA device would snap into the screw which would then pick up vibrations from noises on his left side. The brain would convert those vibrations into sound which would be heard through the right ear. The doctor gave John a trial BAHA that gives similar results to the real BAHA. However, after giving the BAHA a try, John decided he was used to being deaf in the left ear and he didn't want to bother with the BAHA. However, this may be an option for the future if he changes his mind. Oh well…it was an interesting option.

Right before our eyes, John's face began to restore. Early in January, he had an appointment for another EMG (nerve test) to see if there had been any improvement with the facial nerve. By this time, John's

184

smile was about twice as wide as when we returned home. The doctor explained, "Anything less than a 10% activity is a very poor prognosis. I'm sorry to tell you, this nerve only has an 8% activity."

I looked at the doctor and indignantly declared, "I really don't care! Look at him!" *So...if it wasn't the facial nerve, could it have been...another miracle?*

From the time I received Gregg Morgan's e-mail back in November regarding the Outstanding Missourian designation, the wheels were in motion for John to be presented the prestigious award from the Missouri House of Representatives.

From: Connie McClellan
Date: January 10, 2007   7:15 PM
Subject: John presented Outstanding Missourian Award

It was an amazing day here in Mid-Missouri. John, Carl, my Mom, and I joined Jane, and my best friend, Jean "Tim" Timby, at State Representative Jeff Harris' office in the Capitol building in Jefferson City. Rep. Harris was so gracious and respectful to all of us. He told us what to expect and explained the order of events, after which we proceeded to the Legislative Assembly hall.

After the invocation, Jeff gave a wonderful introduction of John, followed by the presentation of the Outstanding Missourian Award to John by Rep. Rod Jetton on behalf of the Missouri State House of Representatives. After that everyone in the room gave John a standing ovation. They said it was the longest standing ovation the House of Representatives has ever received. Wow...what a day...I'll never forget it as long as I live!

From there we were escorted to the Governor's office where we were able to meet Gov. Matt Blunt and have our pictures taken with him in his office, which, by the way, is an amazing room.

Love to all, Connie

From: Connie McClellan
Date: January 10, 2007 10:15 PM
Subject: St. Louis Post Dispatch Article Marine honored on House Floor

186

This was on the St. Louis Post Dispatch online newspaper tonight.

Also, I meant to relay after the presentation of John's award, he had a television interview. The reporter asked what John thought about Gov. Blunt being a Navy man. John didn't skip a beat and said, "Well...Nobody's perfect." Before the interview was broadcast, the interviewer made the comment that John hadn't lost his sense of humor. I just hope Gov. Blunt hasn't lost his! LOL...TOO FUNNY!

Love to all, Connie

From: Connie McClellan
Date: January 11, 2007 16:01:00
Subject: E-mail from Col. Jerry Butter,

Deputy Chief of Staff, Antiterrorism
Marine Corps Forces Central Command

JOHN (UNITED STATES MARINE CORP) FACING OFF WITH
MISSOURI GOVERNOR MATT BLUNT (UNITED STATES NAVY),
JANUARY 10, 2007.

187

Re: John's Outstanding Missourian Award

Dear McClellan Family,

SGM Conti, from the VA Hospital in Tampa, fwd'd
this news to me.

I had the privilege to meet y'all in November (for the
Marine Corps Birthday).

I tell our fellow Americans at every opportunity that
young American Marines (your son among them)
are simply breathtaking. Freedom has a price, but as
long as Marines like John are with us, we will be Free.

Thank you for your service. Please give my greetings to your son.

Semper Fidelis,
Col Jeffry Butter
Deputy Chief of Staff, Antiterrorism
Marine Corps Forces Central Command
COM 813-827-7079/7117/7080
ButterJS@marcent.usmc.mil

25

January 14, 2007 – February 1, 2007

From: Connie McClellan
Date: January 14, 2007 6:01 AM
John's eyebrow moved!

Well...I hope I don't bore you with ANOTHER MIRACLE!

189

Friday, we took John to the V.A. in St. Louis for an evaluation so he can get his therapy extended. They were astounded at his progress.

But here's the REALLY exciting news. We stayed at my best friend Tim's house (Aunt Tim to John). We had dinner and were sitting around the table and John said, "Mom! I just felt my left eyebrow move!" Oh my GOSH! It DID, ever so slightly, but it DID move!...just another miracle... lol (Just kidding! Not JUST another miracle...praise God... ANOTHER miracle!) And the hits (miracles) just keeping on comin'!

Love to all,
Connie

Overall, good news from Haditha...

Re: News from Haditha
1/15/2007 8:59:43 PM
From: David Kelm

Mrs. McClellan,

First, I must apologize for my less than timely replies to your e-mails. Know that I read all of your e-mails, and we all keep up with John's progress thanks to your writings and the efforts of 1stSgt Atkins. The whole company gets to read (and see thanks to your pics) about John's progress, especially his recent award from the State House, what an honor (and truly well-deserved).

190

The platoon continues to do well. The unfortunate exception to this is LCpl William Burke, an assault man who has been with the platoon. He fell and broke his leg in a non-combat related injury the other day. He's absolutely fine, but due to the intense rehabilitation program associated with such an injury, he won't be back to us before we leave. On a good note, Travis Zabroski was recently promoted meritoriously to corporal for his excellent achievements out here. Also, Eduards Primera (Doc Primera) was recently awarded for his lifesaving actions with SSgt Marcus Wilson following his IED strike.

We continue to rotate between missions that include guard force here at the base, patrolling out in town and engaging the locals, and manning traffic checkpoints. As you obviously already know (judging from the article that you forwarded), the berm we've built and the coinciding traffic control measures that we have enacted have made for a much safer Haditha than John knew. We constantly find weapons caches (large amounts of weapons and bomb-making materiel hidden underground and in houses), and it's obvious that the enemy is reeling. Capt Tracy continues to provide creative leadership and motivation, and the new Iraqi Police continue to prove their worth by leading to the arrest of many high-value insurgents.

Otherwise, things continue to be uneventful (which is good!). Please continue to keep me posted on John's progress! I forget which pictures I've already sent to you, but I've enclosed a few of John's squad for him. I hope to talk to you all soon. God bless.

Sincerely yours,
David Kelm

191

1/25/2007 2:53:48AM
From: Darryl Atkins
Subject: News from Haditha

Connie,

Thanks so much. I'm glad things are coming along well for you and the family. The enemy is ramping up and changing tactics again. We had some Marines get terribly wounded a few days ago but thank God they weren't killed. The staff has been busy keeping the Marines minds on the task at hand: to continue to close with and destroy the enemy. We want to ensure that no one becomes complacent.

Even though things have slowed down here, they (the Marines) have to understand that this is one of the most dangerous places in the world. It's weird to think that we would have to keep their minds in the game. Initially getting here, it was almost all out war everyday. Now we only get hit every now and then young Marines minds begin to wander; thinking about going home and they get bored. Plus, we do a lot of things like trying to help get the hospital up in running and other improvements in the city. They lose focus. We will continue to push them until our time is over here.

Thanks for the number. Take care.

1stSgt D. L. Atkins
Echo Company 2/3
Haditha City, Iraq

192

Hard pressed on my right. My center is yielding. Impossible to maneuver. Situation excellent. I am attacking. -Ferdinand Foch- at the Battle of the Marne

From: Connie McClellan
Date: January 25, 2007   6:15 AM
Subject: E-mail from John's 1st Sgt.

Thank you, Lord, that you are helping John's buds to stay focused on the task at hand, and on keeping safe and that You are protecting them every minute of every day, keeping Your angels watching over them constantly. We thank You that You are bringing them home safe and whole in every way, in Jesus' name we pray. Amen.
Love to all, Connie

From: Connie McClellan
Date: January 31, 2007 6:20 AM
Subject: John's Dimple is BACK!

See the attached picture! What do you see on the left side of John's face? YES! YES! His DIMPLE is back! I KNEW it would! I knew it WOULD!

When I was pregnant with John, I told Carl, "I'd give anything if this baby had dimples...but nobody in your family has dimples and I've only got one sister with dimples. I would love it if this baby had dimples."

I wasn't praying for him to have dimples, I just made the comment. Well...when he was born he had...30 dimples! One on each cheek, two on each elbow, two on each knee, one on each finger and one on each toe. God responded to my comment ...BIG TIME!

193

Eventually, of course, the dimples all dissipated except the ones on his face. And, when he got shot, the one on the left side of his face disappeared along with every other muscle on that side. But I knew God was going to give me that dimple back, and He DID! Also, you will note that John's smile is 95% complete., and his eye totally closes, so we don't have to use the "goop" at all!. Praise the Lord! Thank you, Jesus!

AND, it's not because the facial nerve has repaired itself as it only has 8% function which gives a very poor prognosis. Could it be ...GOD!? Please share in our joy on the eve of John's 21st birthday.

Love, Connie

P.S. We go in on Monday to see the eye doctor to see when we can get the gold weight out of his eye. I told him, "John, now that your eye is closing, we need to see when we can get that gold weight out, because...I need a new necklace...lol." He said, "MOM! I NEED A NEW NECKLACE!" lol. I said, "But John...after all that I've been through!?" Anyway, we've had some fun with that.

194

JOHN'S DIMPLE IS BACK, JANUARY 13, 2007

26

February 2, 2007 – March 17, 2007

The bad news continues from Haditha...

195

February 2, 2007 7:34:22 AM
From: Trent Smith's Dad
Subject: Matt Bradford

Does John know Matt Bradford? He is in Bethesda
with terrible wounds from an IED. Here's the story
below:
http://www.progress-index.com/site/news.cfm?ne
wsid=17781782&BRD=2271&PAG=461&dept_
id=462946&rfi=6

Smitty's Dad

From: Connie McClellan
Date: February 4, 2007   7:36 AM
Subject: E-mail about Matt Bradford, from John's platoon

Matt lost both legs from an IED and is at Bethesda National Naval Center, which was the same hospital that John was in. See below for the link to an article about him.

Thank you, Lord, that you are with Matt and his family and that Matt will recover totally and be able to use his prosthetics successfully and with amazing adaptability speed. Touch him in a mighty way, Lord, and let him know that you are there for him, in Jesus' name. Amen.

Love to all,
Connie

196

I asked John if he remembered Matt Bradford. He thought he knew Matt, but had difficulty picturing him. This scenario was typical of some of the memory problems John endured.

As we continued with John's therapy and recovery, life in Haditha continued to be dangerous and harrowing for our boys. The fear those boys have lived with on a daily basis was hard to imagine.

RE: 2/3 injuries
2/12/2007 8:23:34 Am
From: Darryl Atkins

Connie,

Glad to see that John is doing better. Let him know that we are still thinking about him and praying for him. We are still fighting the battle over here. I'm thoroughly convinced that we will fight these guys until the day we leave. They have started concentrating on more IED attacks and guys running around with suicide vests. It's pretty scary stuff but we are coping with it. On a sad note, let him know that LCpl's Dominguez and Bravo where hit with an IED strike. They are both all right. Dominguez has a compound fracture in his lower leg and Bravo got some frag around his right eye (he can still see), plus frag hits on his arms and legs. They are in Germany right now and will be sent to KBay when they get a couple of surgeries done. It's a damn shame when that type of news is good news. Nobody died. God is good.

197

1stSgt D. L. Atkins
Echo Company 2/3
Haditha City, Iraq

From: Connie McClellan
Date: February 12, 2007 7:10 PM
Subject: E-mail from John's First Sgt.

Thank you, Lord that you are healing these boys completely, totally, and that you are giving their families everything they need to get through the ordeal, in Jesus' name. Amen

As we settled into our routine, more and more, our lives were starting to return to normal: John with his therapy regimen, and Carl and I with our resumed roles as insurance agents. John's progress proved to be steady.

From: Connie McClellan
Date: February 12, 2007   8;10 PM
Subject: Update on John's progress

Well, it's been awhile since I've written regarding John's progress. As you might expect it is not as dramatic as it's been in the past 4 months, but it's still dramatic to us! His smile is still growing and is, I would say, 95-98% restored. His dimple is SO apparent! (As you know, I'm thrilled about that!)

198

Wednesday, he goes to the eye doctor to see when we can get the gold weight out. It may be that they'll suggest he have it done in Bethesda when we go back to get his skullcap put back on. That is March 21st, by the by. I wasn't sure if I gave you that information yet or not. Carl, John & I will be leaving on 3/19. We have the pre-op activity on 3/20, surgery on 3/21, and then...hopefully... prayerfully...we'll only need to be there a few days for recovery which would put us back here on or about 3/25.

Please pray:

Thank you, Lord that John's surgery will go perfectly and that his recovery will be speedy. And, thank you, Lord, as his buds begin the downhill trek for coming home that you bring them home safe and whole in everyway, physically, emotionally, psychologically and spiritually in Jesus' name. Amen.

I realize we're still more than a month away from his surgery, but, in my opinion, you just can't start praying too early or too much, so...get used to seeing the above prayer...

Love to all,

Connie

P.S. John went with one of his old friends, Peter Stoops, to the Mizzou vs. Kansas game on Saturday. They got to sit in the hoity-toity, glassed-in box-suite with the good food and drinks. The bad news is that Mizzou got stomped. The good news is that, at half time, they put the camera on John (viewed on the overhead scoreboard thingy), told everyone who he was and what he has done, and then the crowd gave him a standing ovation. How cool is that?

199

I asked him what he did. He said he just smiled and gave them the "Miss America" rotating wrist wave. I said, "You're kidding, right?" (about the wave). Fortunately...he said, 'Yes.''..lol...what a jokester he is! Yes, the joy is back...thank you, Jesus!

From: Connie McClellan
Date: February 14, 2007 7:00 PM
Subject: John in Gears of War competition

You aren't going to believe this! Last night John and a friend of his participated in a Gears of War (video game) competition! They didn't win, but they played for a while before they were eliminated. I thought that was pretty good! I mean, how many people do YOU know who were shot in the head and 5 months later are playing in a video game competition?! lol...okay, okay, so you only know one person who got a headshot and survived, but really...think about it!

Anyway...very cool, don't you think?

Love to all,
Connie

From: Connie McClellan
Sent: March 13, 2007 14:02:00
Subject: John moved out today!

Do you believe it? Six months ago he was shot in the head and today he's living on his own. (Yesterday, he moved in with two of his best friends, since like, the first grade. I am in awe...God is so good!)

We leave on Sunday to return to Bethesda National Naval Medical Center for John's cranioplasty (skull replacement surgery). While we're there, they're going to give him tests to be sure that his left eye closes all the way. If it does, they should be able to take out the gold weight out of his left eyelid. I have relinquished all rights to the gold weight

and will not seek custody for my necklace....lol....
John's going to do something very cool with it for
himself...that's fine....lol....

He's still doing Rusk Rehab in the mornings. The
progress is not as dramatic, but it's still steady.
We're VERY encouraged!

Love to all, Connie

When John first announced he was moving out, I had mixed emotions as I still worried about him in many ways. The possibility of him hitting the back of his head where there was no skull was always disconcerting, as well as the usual parental concerns of whether he was eating right, getting enough rest, etc. Also, Carl and I had a tendency to hound him with, "John, you need to work on your memory skills." Or, reminiscent of when he was younger, "John, you're spending too much time playing video games." Or, "John you need to eat this, or that." In retrospect, when he moved out we were all "woo hooing!" Being "at home" again after having been on his own had been trying for all of us.

201

27

March 18, 2007 – March 24, 2007

Our next scheduled event was returning to Bethesda for John's cranioplasty. On Sunday, March 18th, we flew from St. Louis to Washington D.C., arriving in Bethesda that evening. As we checked into the Navy Lodge once again, we experienced déjà vu ... albeit, a good déjà vu, that is. Truly, our previous Bethesda experience had been a good one in every sense, as every day took us to a higher level of John's recovery.

As we approached our room at the Navy Lodge, we felt as though we were home again. This time we were in a room on the 1st floor; however it had the exact design and layout as our previous room. This room worked especially well for Carl as he only had to walk ten feet to the smoking area.

On Monday, we walked to NNMC where we were scheduled for an 8:00 AM appointment with Dr. Lindsay, the ENT surgeon who had inserted the gold weight in John's eyelid. No sooner had we taken a seat in the waiting room when we were called into the examining room. Two minutes later, Dr. Lindsay entered. Obviously, what she saw pleased her as immediately she had the most exuberant look on her face.

"You don't need that weight any longer," she told John. Then, addressing Carl and me, "I can tell by the crow's feet next to his eye that the eye is closing completely."

I quipped, "Well, John, there it is! You want crow's feet and I don't!"

Dr. Lindsay scheduled the weight-removing, outpatient surgery for the following Monday.

Immediately following the ENT appointment, we met with Ellen Crown the public relations director for NNMC. Ellen arranged for us to have an interview with an American journalist employed by Al Jazeera, the Arabic news and satellite TV channel.

Our interview was to be included in an Al Jazeera project designed to give the Iraqi people a more humanistic view of our Marines and soldiers, as real people with families who care about them.

That afternoon was sunny, but chilly. This time of year, Carl's old, favorite smoking section was located on the side of the hotel where the sun wasn't. Earlier, I noticed another smoking area on the sunny side of the hotel. We decided that would be a more comfortable place for Carl to satisfy his nicotine craving. We had never been to this area.

In fact, until this time, we were unaware of its existence. Ten minutes after we sat down, a woman joined us.

We introduced ourselves and then repeated the same old question, "Who are you here for, and why are they here?" Her name was Terri and she and her sister had been at Bethesda since mid-February with her Marine nephew, Matt, who lost both legs and the sight in his left eye as a result of an IED explosion. At the time, his right eye also had no sight; however the doctors were hopeful that his right eyesight would be restored.

We told her about John and explained we were here for his cranioplasty. She asked, "Where was John stationed when he was injured?"

"Haditha, Iraq."

She exclaimed, "Haditha? That's where Matt was injured!"

"What company Matt was with?" I asked.

"Two-Three Echo."

"Two-Three ECHO! That was John's company! What's Matt's last name?"

"Bradford"

"Matt Bradford?! Oh my Gosh! We've been praying for him since we first received the e-mail back in February!!"

I couldn't believe it! This was SO God! Had we not landed in that new smoking section at that precise time, we wouldn't have met Terri and wouldn't have discovered Matt was at the hospital.

Immediately, I rushed back to the room to tell John. We felt an urgency to see Matt as Terri relayed he would be leaving first thing in the morning for Richmond,

Virginia to begin his rehabilitation. Without hesitation, we returned to the hospital where John immediately recognized Matt when we walked into his room.

What an incredibly, positive attitude this young man had. Matt was noticeably grateful for the visit, even though he couldn't see John. He told us how much it meant for the guys in his unit to learn that John had not only lived but was recovering so well.

While he appeared resolved to the loss of his legs and left eye, he expressed his fear that his right eye might not restore.

Early the next morning, we returned again to see Matt before his 9:00 departure. During this visit, I had an opportunity to pray with him.

Later in the afternoon we launched the paperwork process for John's cranioplasty scheduled for the next day. In addition, John had various blood tests performed.

205

From: Connie McClellan
Date: March 20, 2007 4:10 PM
Subject: NNMC reunion with 5th floor nurse.

We were running around the hospital on Tuesday doing everything needed for our surgery on Wednesday. At one point, we were standing in front of the elevator on the second floor when a nurse started to walk past us. She suddenly stopped and started squealing "Oh my God! Oh my God! I can't believe it! Look at you! Oh my God!" And then she started crying!

She was our nurse on the 5th floor back in October. She was SO adorable! Then, she said to John, "You HAVE to come back to see nurse 'so and so'" (can't remember her name). "She will FLIP when she sees you." So, we went back to the 2nd floor ward and saw Nurse 'so and so'. They were SO thrilled to see John's improvement. They're like, "You have no idea how important this is to us."

...talk about a HUGE warm fuzzy!

Okay, here's why I interpret this as another touch from God. These two nurses WERE on the 5th floor when we knew them. Since that time they have moved to the 2nd floor. If this nurse had not walked by us during that 30 sec window while we were waiting for the elevator, we would not have seen her as we have not reason to be on the 2nd floor ward. Coincidence? I don't think so!

Love to all, Connie

206

On Tuesday we ran out of time before we could complete all of the paperwork for John's surgery scheduled for the next morning. As a result, Dr. Armonda's nurse asked that we come back Wednesday morning at 6:45. This would allow the needed time to complete the paperwork prior to John's surgery.

Wednesday morning we arose bright and early for our 6:45 AM appointment. Carl persisted in rushing us to get to the appointment. John and I weren't paying attention to the time; we were just hurrying as fast as we could to keep up with Carl. Upon our arrival at Dr.

207

Armonda's office, I looked at my watch and saw that it was only 6:20. "Carl!" I growled. "It's only 6:20!"

"I know," he retorted, "Our appointment's at 6:30."

"No, it's not! It's not until 6:45!" In my opinion, every minute at that hour of the day was valuable time that we could have spent in bed.

He apologized for rushing us unnecessarily, as we proceeded to the uninhabited waiting area which was still dark. The lights weren't scheduled to come on for another 25 minutes. Well...one moment I was cussing Carl, and the next moment I was kissing him because...

we weren't there two minutes when, Dr. Armonda walked through the waiting room on his way to his office. "What are you doing here so early?" he asked.

I responded with a chuckle, "Don't ask."

From: Connie McClellan
Sent: March 21, 2007 09:37:00
Subject: John Didn't Have to Have His Cranioplasty!

208

We went to neurosurgery this morning early, so we could complete the paperwork. This was a good thing, because Dr. Armonda arrived shortly after we did, so we caught him coming in. He hadn't seen John yet, so when he saw John he said, "Let's take a look and see how you're doing."

He looked at John's head and asked if he had any pain. John said he didn't. Then, Dr. Armonda said, "We don't need to do this surgery. The muscle behind his head has formed well enough that it is providing the protection that is needed." If his skull were gone further on top of his head, then we wouldn't have that option, but as it is, he does not need the cranioplasty. We were so stunned, we just all stood there with our mouths open. What a riot!

After about five seconds, I said, "So what I'm hearing you say is, that.......... we don't EVER have to have this surgery?"

He said, "That's right."

Oh my gosh! You could have blown us all over with a feather! THANK YOU, JESUS! We were

SOOOOOOOOOO relieved! John was especially relieved, as unbeknownst to us, he didn't sleep at all the night before in anticipation of this surgery and its aftereffects.

Thank you so much for your prayers. We had the best answer to prayer that we could hope for.

So, now...all we have to wait on his eye surgery on Monday. Since this is basically an outpatient procedure, I am looking to come back this weekend and have Carl stay with John and return as scheduled on Wednesday. Wow...

Anyway, that's where we are for the moment. Is that good news or what?!?

Love to all, Connie

209

Had Carl not been confused on the timing of the appointment, we would not have caught Dr. Armonda coming into work, and wouldn't have had that "divine" meeting.

All along, I had been praying that the surgery go well, that the recovery be miraculously quick and minimally painful. It didn't dawn on me to pray that he wouldn't have to have it at all! God definitely had a better plan in this situation!

The next day, Thursday, March 22nd, I expressed to John, "God has given us this time. Do you remember that young Marine who came to visit us while we were on the 5th floor last October? You know the one that took the two mortar rounds to the chest?"

"Yeah, I remember."

"What do you think about going back to the hospital and doing for those soldiers what that soldier who took the mortar rounds did for us."

"I'd like that."

So, we did. We returned to the 5th floor and met with the charge nurse, who also remembered us from last October. We asked if it would be okay if we visited with some of the soldiers.

"*Yes! Oh yes!*" She exclaimed. "You go back and visit with the soldier in room 2808 and then come back here and I'll give you your next assignment." She was very enthusiastic, which confirmed to us we were doing the right thing.

Time allowed us to visit with five soldiers. Several of them had just arrived from Iraq, so their families weren't there yet. They were especially appreciative of our visit and were very impressed with John and his progress. John and I both felt we had really made a difference in those boys' lives. What a rewarding experience...for everyone involved!

Friday morning we took the subway into Washington. Previously, we arranged to meet with our United States Representative, Kenny Hulshof; you know, the one who could have been my brother? Representative Hulshof presented John with a flag that had flown over the capital that day for an hour, in honor of John.

After concluding our visit with Rep Hulshof, we were taken on a tour of the Capital by one of Senator Kit Bond's assistants. That day will go down in the McClellan memory book in a mighty way.

211

From: Connie McClellan
Sent: Saturday, March 24, 2007 10:11 AM
Subject: A Visit with "Uncle Kenny"

I don't think I ever relayed this, but in September, when John first arrived at Bethesda, our U.S. House of Representative, Kenny Hulshof had tried to visit John at the NNMC hospital (before we arrived). Because he wasn't a relative, they would not let him up to see John. I heard this from Rep. Hulshof's assistant. At that time, I told him, "He should have told him he was my brother!" We laughed.

The next day, as Carl & I were leaving the Columbia airport for Bethesda, Rep Hulshof's plane was arriving as we were waiting for our plane. We talked briefly and I reiterated my suggestion that

"You should have told them you were my brother."
We laughed. Later I told John that story.

Yesterday, we were able to visit, Rep. Hulshof at
his office at the Capitol. As we walked in and were
greeted by him, John said, "Hi, Uncle Kenny!" We
ALL laughed! Kenny knew right away what that
was all about. Too funny!

We visited with him for about an hour and then,
one of Sen. Bond's assistants led us on a tour of
the Capitol. We got to sit in while the Senate was
debating some issues. It was SOOOOOOOOOO
interesting!

Love to all, Connie

28

April 6, 2007 – May 26, 2007

After we returned from Bethesda, John resumed his therapy at Rusk Rehab as Carl and I donned our insurance agents' hats. Finally, our lives had a semblance of normalcy until...

From: Connie McClellan
Subject: John has had a seizure
Date: Fri, 06 Apr 2007 12:39:15 -0400

Soon after John got to Rusk this morning he had a seizure. He is at UMC hospital getting tests done.

Please pray with me. Thank you, Lord, that this seizure has NOT caused any problems and WILL NOT reoccur, in Jesus' name. Amen.

About the only thing we can figure is that yesterday he had jogged a mile and this morning he had lifted some heavy trash bags, so he may not be as ready for that activity as what we thought. Anyway...don't stop praying until I tell you!

I'll keep you informed as soon as I know what's going on.

Love Connie

**From: Connie McClellan
Sent: April 6, 2007 9:20 PM
Reflections on John's seizure**

You know, as I reflect on the day's events, I am so grateful that John had his seizure at Rusk, rather than at home. At Rusk, all of the resources needed were immediately available to give him the treatment that he needed. Thank you, LORD!
I KNOW that I KNOW that John's going to be okay. I also know that all things work for good.

Thank you for praying: Thank you, Lord, in the name of Jesus that John is restored totally and completely. Amen.

Love to all, Connie

**From: Connie McClellan
Date: April 7, 2007
Subject: Information about John's second seizure**

Through miscommunication (+ lousy documentation by the night nurse at the hospital) we were led to believe that John had a second seizure last night. As a result, they kept him an extra day for observation.

Well! I just found out that he did NOT have a second seizure... PRAISE THE LORD! He was kept an extra day for no reason, but that's OKAY! As long as he didn't have the second seizure, I DON'T CARE! The difference between having one seizure only and having two within an 18 hour period is HUGE! THANK YOU, JESUS!

Thank you all for your continued prayers!

Love to all! Connie

P.S. Happy Easter!

After John had his seizure at Rusk Rehabilitation Center, we spent the better part of the day in the University Hospital emergency room. Throughout the time in the emergency room, John was extremely disoriented and confused. The nurse began to ask him a series of questions starting with, "What year is it?"

215

To that John responded, "2002?"

Increasingly, I felt uneasy as I listened to the remainder of his inaccurate responses. Finally, they admitted him into the hospital for observation to be sure the anti-seizure medication they gave him was working.

I returned home for the night. As soon as I awoke the next morning, I called the hospital. "How did John get along last night?" I asked his morning charge nurse who had just come on duty.

"I'm sorry to tell you," she reluctantly relayed, "John had another seizure during the night."

"*What?* What happened?"

"According to his chart, the night nurse had given him Ativan because he had another seizure."

"Have you been in to see him this morning?"

"Yes, I was just in with him?"

"How did he seem? Was he alert? Was he lucid?"

"He seemed fine."

"So, what happened with the seizure?"

"I'm not sure; all the chart shows is that he had a seizure around midnight and the nurse gave him Ativan."

"Don't you think that's strange? I mean yesterday he had a seizure and after being given Ativan, was totally out of it for at least twelve hours. Now, it's only seven hours after his seizure and Ativan and he's perfectly fine?" We both agreed the whole scenario made no sense.

When the doctors came in for their rounds, I asked for the details surrounding John's seizure. They advised they weren't exactly sure themselves because the documentation from the night nurse was extremely vague. Also, the night nurse didn't call the doctors when it happened. Hospital protocol for patients who have seizures was to always call the in-house doctor. At this point, we were all questioning, "Did he really have a seizure?" This was an important question, as the difference between having one seizure and two in twenty-four hours (with medication) was huge. It made the difference between John continuing to live on his own or having to bring him home with us.

The doctors promised to investigate. Two hours later, they returned to John's room and broke the news. "We have not been able to contact the night nurse, but from everything we can surmise, it appears that John did have another seizure. Consequently, we'll need to keep him for another night for observation."

Needless to say, we were devastated.

That night, after I arrived home, I called the hospital for one last check before I went to bed. Much to my surprise the nurse who answered the phone was the elusive night nurse from the previous night.

Excitedly and with much anticipation, I asked, "So, what happened last night with John's seizure?"

"Oh," he replied, "he didn't have a seizure."

"What? Then what happened?"

"Well, there was this patient on the floor who was yelling and carrying on and it scared John, so I gave him the medication."

HA! Don't you read the newspapers? Obviously, you don't know who John is! Nothing scares him! This doesn't add up.

Immediately I called John, "Do you remember being scared by someone screaming on the floor last night?"

"Uh, nooooooooo."

At the hospital the next morning, I corralled the morning charge nurse and repeated my conversation with the night nurse. I explained, "Okay, I'm not going to make a big deal out of this, as this is an internal problem that the hospital needs to investigate.

217

However, I do demand three things:

1.) John is to be the first patient on the doctors' roster this morning.

2.) John is to be discharged within the hour.

3.) Tri-Care, the military insurance company, will NOT be charged for the second night that John was forced to stay at the hospital.

She replied, "I'm on it!" Her efforts paid off as all three demands were met.

That morning, I learned that Ativan, the medication the night nurse "gave" John, was a highly abused drug. Immediately, I suspected the night nurse *said* he administered it, when he probably kept it for himself. When I suggested this theory to the doctors, they assured me they would investigate the situation.

218

One day in August, 2007, John and I stopped at a gas station and just happened to run into John's charge nurse from the hospital.

She asked, "Hey, you know that night nurse who said he gave John the Ativan that night in the hospital?"

"Yeah?"

"Well," she continued, "one day the police came in, handcuffed him, went to his locker and found a whole bunch of drugs that he had stolen from the hospital!"

I felt vindicated, but at the same time I felt pity for someone so desperate for drugs that he would risk his job, not to mention his freedom once he goes to jail.

.

From: Connie McClellan
Date: April 7, 2007
Subject: John is out of the hospital

John is out of the hospital and back home with his roommates

He was discharged from the hospital this morning and is back at home with the guys. Please pray: Thank you, Lord, that you continue to protect John every minute of every day, and protect him from any further seizures, in Jesus' name. Amen.

Happy Easter EVERYONE!
Connie

From: Connie McClellan
Date: 4/11/07
John's buds are back from Iraq

219

Thank you, Lord, that John's buds are back. Thank you, Lord, for the families of the boys that did not make it, that you give them your peace that surpasses all understanding, and give them the assurance to know that they will see them again.... in heaven.

Thank you, Lord, that Post Traumatic Stress in NOT an issue with the boys who have returned, and they are whole in every way, emotionally, psychologically, physically and spiritually, in Jesus' precious name we pray.

PHEW! Now, we can ALL breathe a sigh of relief!

John is to fly out of St. Louis on Saturday to be

reunited with his buds. What a photo op that will be! My only regret is that I'M NOT HOLDING THE CAMERA!.....lol He will return on 4/22.

Please pray:

Thank you, Lord, that John's trip will be perfect and he will have no problems, in Jesus' name. Amen.

Love to all, Connie

Praise God, John's unit had returned to Hawaii...

Date: April 12, 2007
From: Dave Lt.Kelm

Well, we're back.

I can't say thank you enough to those of you who offered your help in any form while we were deployed. As I mentioned, your packages, cards, letters, and thoughts and prayers really helped my Marines by letting them know that so many people cared about them and supported them. Additionally, and more realistically, we didn't have too many amenities available to us in the beginning, and they loved just getting some stuff to snack on.

Although I can't thank everyone, please know that every letter, card, package or anything you sent went to a Marine who needed it.

As far as what we did in Haditha, the results speak for themselves. In September/October, we were attacked constantly by mortars, IEDs, snipers, and small arms fire, and the police force had a grand total of

10 officers. During Ramadan, our company would be attacked up to 15 times a day. I've been on three-hour patrols that would see contact three times before coming back in the wire. People would go out of their way to avoid patrols in the streets, sometimes people would shake just from having Marines in their houses, and the mention of anybody joining the police force almost without exception got the women of the house balling their faces off. The murder and intimidation was just that effective. Even the mayor of Haditha was a known terrorist who had gone into hiding and was wanted by us. The city still had water, electricity, and other services, but there was no government; the insurgents literally ran the town. Haditha was one of the most dangerous places in Iraq (haha, I can tell you that now that I'm back).

221

Now, Haditha has a police force over 200 strong and counting, with a steady trickle of continuing recruits. Government workers are actually working again. Contractors are working with Marines to improve the infrastructure. Sheikhs and former government/military officials are publicly working with the new city government (we found/arrested the old mayor in December) and police force. Every single market and school in town is open again, and even teenage girls are going to school now. Oh, and my platoon hasn't been attacked since the beginning of February, how boring is that? Attacks on Marines/IP went from 15 per day to a current pace of about a handful per month. If you want to know more, a few reporters have been to Haditha and wrote of the progress (if you want to find them try searching for something like "Haditha Echo Company" to avoid getting tons of articles about the massacre).

But anyway, this e-mail's getting too long. That's what my company's been up to. As for me, thanks to all of you who sent e-mails, packages, cards, letters, and kept me in your thoughts and prayers. Thanks especially to my family for answering the phone those few times I called and always let me know how much they cared. However, I needed far less support than the Marines, as I was offered daughters in marriage and even someone's baby (I swear to God). Needless to say, Mulazim Dawud is pretty well set up in Haditha if this insurgency thing dies down. Also thanks to Roscoe my life advisor for running my entire life outside of Iraq while I was deployed and for setting up my leave arrangements.

I'm indebted to so many people for so much help. Thanks again for everyone's support, and (for those lucky few of you), I'll see you soon.

-Dave

P.S. You wouldn't have been worried if you just would've accepted the fact that I'm invincible.

222

The Marines provided John's transportation back to Hawaii to be with his buds after they returned from Iraq. He was actually supposed to leave a week earlier, but with the seizure, we thought it best to wait a few days to be sure he didn't have any more problems with the seizures.

From: Connie McClellan
Sent: Apr 13, 2007 4:24 AM
John leaves for Hawaii TOMORROW!

Good Morning everyone!

John is VERY excited to be leaving tomorrow morning for Hawaii to meet with his buds. BUT I don't think he's half as excited as they are for him to arrive. They arrived earlier this week.

Please pray: Thank you, Lord, that John's trip to and from HI will be uneventful as far as his flights and his physical well being. Thank you that this is going to be the reunion of reunions with his buds. Thank you, Lord, that his buds are whole in every way, spiritually, emotionally, mentally and physically, in Jesus' name. Amen.

AND pray for me, cause I'm the one getting him to the airport by 5:00 AM...ha!. We're leaving this evening to go to St. Louis to spend the night at John's "Aunt Tim's" house in the Central West End of St. Louis. That way, we only have to get up at 4:00 AM rather than 2:00 AM...agggggggggghhhhhhhh...but it's worth it! My only regret is that I'm not going to be there with him...lol.

Love to all,

Connie

I have to admit, of all the things that I've been through since John's injury, putting him on that plane to Hawaii proved to be one of the most difficult. The combination of John's short term memory loss and the importance of his remembering to take his anti-seizure

223

medication three times a day, created an uneasy feeling for me when I dropped him off at the airport.

Of course, I took the necessary precautions. I bought him a medical necklace, and put his condition, meds, and my phone number on it. But most importantly, one more time, I gave it to God. I prayed, "Lord, I can't be there with him. You're the only one that can be with him at all times. Watch over him, keep him safe, remind him to take his meds, keep him seizure-free."

From: Connie McClellan
Date: 4/24/07
Subject: John's back from Hawaii!

I wanted to give you an update on John. He arrived home on Sunday. He had a great time. Did he take any pictures? NOOOOOOOOOOOOOOOOOOOOO! Would he give me a play by play of the reunion? NOOOOOOOOOOOOOOO!

So, anyway...that's all I know to tell you...lol... but he is home safe and sound and had no problems... woohoo!

Love, Connie

From: Connie McClellan
Sent: Monday, May 07, 2007 5:54 PM
Subject: Guess what?! John's going to be a DAD!

He's picking up his new Golden Retriever puppy on June 1st!

You'll NEVER guess what he's going to name it? Okay...you probably guessed it...LUCKY! I'm going to have a GRAND-DOG! I'm not sure who's more excited...him or me! He's finally getting that dog I would never let him have, because I didn't want the responsibility or the mess. NOW! John has his own place, and his good friend, Ryan, who is also his landlord, says he can have a DOG! I'm so excited. Just 'cause I wouldn't let him have one doesn't mean I don't LOVE dogs, because I DO! Especially Golden Retrievers!

We went on Saturday to meet Lucky; he's 2 ½ weeks old. And of course, we wanted to meet his parents. They are beautiful! They are the golden red color.

Then, tomorrow, John is going to start taking guitar lessons. That would be another way that I'm glad he has his own place...lol...God Bless his roommates Ryan and Jake! ...lol

225

Anyway, that's what's going on in our world.

We went on Friday for EEG. We'll know the results of that this week.

Love to all, Connie
From: Connie McClellan
DATE: May 23, 2007
Subject: E-mail from Dave Kelm

Hey Connie,

It's good to continue to hear of all the amazing things

happening to John. It was great to finally see him again when he came out here to Hawaii. I was sorry that you couldn't make it, I was looking forward to meeting you. Your updates have been so helpful, and so many great people have contacted me because of you.

Anyway, have fun this weekend and may God continue to bless you and your family!

-Dave

Every year Columbia hosts a Salute to Veterans Air Show, which always honors various veterans. This year's Salute to Veterans asked John to be an honored guest, and he accepted.

The weekend began with a special skeet shooting competition for the honored guests. For John to be able to participate in this event, was a miracle in itself...shot in the head in September...shooting instead in May. The weekend culminated with the Air Show parade and banquet in which the honored guests were presented. That weekend served as another incredible entry for the McClellan memory book.

From: Connie McClellan
Date: May 26, 2007
Subject: John Mac and Miracle # 21, or is it 22 or... 24? I've lost COUNT!

As you all know with John's injury, the vision in his left eye has not been good. The hope was that once that gold weight was removed that the eyeball

JOHN WITH GOLDEN RETRIEVER PUPPY, LUCKY. 5/30/07

227

JOHN WITH FACE RESTORED

JOHN WITH COUSINS LANCE AND LARRY LOETHEN IN EDINBOROUGH, SCOTLAND, JULY, 2007. (THIS IS THE "SEQUEL" TO THE PICTURE ON PAGE 111, TAKEN IN OCTOBER, 2006 WITH LANCE AND LARRY AT NNMC)

would resume it's original shape removing the astigmatism that they hoped was the cause of the blurriness.

WELL! The eye test yesterday showed...20/20 in BOTH EYES! THANK YOU JESUS!

The irony in all this, is that when we received the call from what I have since dubbed "the good day" (September 28th), the doctors explained that John's condition had done a '180' from the day before. However, they went on to relay that one of the real concerns was that John might be blind...ha!...didn't have to do blind! Quite, the contrary, because God had a MUCH better plan!

Anyway, I wanted you ALL to share in our joy! BIG day in Columbia, MO yesterday! Praise the Lord!

Thank you, Lord, that you have healed John's eyesight 100%, just as we asked, in Jesus' name. Amen.

Love to all, Connie

229

29

In Summary...

From the day we learned of John's injury, I began believing God would restore him to 100%. John is not there yet, but he continues to improve. I truly believe that he is still God's work in progress. Following are the three deficiencies for which we are still praying:

1.) Short term memory restored to 100%.
2.) Hearing in left ear restored.
3.) John to be seizure free with no anti-seizure medications needed.

I know dealing with these deficiencies has to be frustrating for John, but truly, you would never know if you were to see him or talk to him. I think he's just grateful to be alive and doing as well as he is, as is everyone who knows him. Often I'll read, hear, or see stories of other traumatic brain injury patients with severe problems. This could have been John. We are so appreciative to God for the 24 + miracles that He has done for John.

In summary, the following is a list of the more pronounced miracles performed by God, each of which represented a serious concern at some point in John's recovery:

1.) He lived
2.) He can see.
3.) He can hear.
4.) He can talk.
5.) He can talk with both vocal chords.
6.) His face is not marred except for a little ½ inch scar in front of his left ear where the bullet entered.
7.) He has no headaches or pain of any kind.
8.) He has no dizziness.
9.) His joy is restored.
10.) His personality is exactly the same as it was before his injuries.
11.) His left hand works perfectly.
12.) He can walk.
13.) He can run.
14.) He's not retarded.
15.) HE'S NOT A VEGETABLE!
16.) The movement in his left eyebrow is restored.
17.) The wrinkle in the left side of his forehead is restored.
18.) His eyelid closes and the weight was removed.
19.) He can read.
20.) He can write.
21.) His full smile and left dimple are restored.
22.) His Cranioplasty surgery was cancelled because

the muscle had grown over the brain sufficiently to protect it.

23.) When he had his seizure, everything was in place to protect him.

24.) Both eyes are 20/20.

What a ride this experience has been. Writing this book gave me the opportunity to reflect and marvel at all the things God did for John, and for Carl and me. God answering the prayers of the people, I believe, has given us the miracle Marine that we have today. And, God is not finished yet, so don't stop praying until I say so!

30

TRIBUTE TO CPL. MARIO ANES

Corporal Mario Anes saved John's life after John sustained the gunshot wound to his head. Mario's mother, Nilda, and I had communicated regularly since her first call to us on October 10th while we were at NNMC. In August 2007, at my request, Nilda asked Mario if he would e-mail the details of what happened that fateful day.

233

From: Mario Anes
To: Nilda Anes
Date: 8/20/07
Subject: Mac

Okay Mom, here we go. It's hard cuz I really don't want to relive that moment of Mac, but I want to do this for his family.

Sept. 26, I believe, it was a pretty quiet morning... we had orders to patrol the south part of Haditha... 11 hundred hours our patrol was set to leave out of spider hole from our base. So we did exactly that, at 1100 we stepped out not knowing that this moment was going to change our lives forever. Mac was in my element, he was my machine gunner and carried the M249 Squad Automatic Weapon. Mac was just behind me cuz I knew that if anything went down, he was gonna be there for me and at the time so he was my personal protection. Well here we go... we stepped off u know patrolling and I'm telling my element every so many steps, "Hey drunk monkey do it!!" Drunk monkey was a phrase we used to tell everyone to zig zag ur route, like stagger everywhere to make ur self a hard target for snipers in the area.

Myself and my other point man, Billy Burke, came across a problem in the route, one which I didn't like...but we had orders, so of course, I said okay, but let's go quickly. Now as we're starting to head into the open area, I turn and say again "Drunk monkey guys, make sure ur doing it!"

234

As Burke and I are about to finish crossing the open area we hear, the loudest bang, pop, whistle, snap in the world. We even saw the tracer to that round scream by us. So I quickly hit the ground and started to crawl on all fours before I got up and ran to a court yard gate. As soon as I gained entry, I started to get accountability of my men. I saw Burke, then Marchitell who was Mac's buddy pair. I yelled at Marchitell, "Where's Mac? His reply was, "I don't know." I ran to the courtyard gate and saw a Marine lying in the open, motionless. I yelled over the radio to Sgt. Davidson, "I think it's Mac, man, holy #%!*!! Mac's down, I'm going to get him." So as soon as I started to run, Burke followed. At the same time, Sgt. Davidson ordered the squad to provide cover and assist me in any way possible to get Mac out of there. Here comes the bad part----- okay----- so ur warned...

As I ran up to Mac, his face was purple/blue and blood was squirting out of his head wound, the one on his face. My first thought was @#%! man he's dead, but never did I give up. I quickly grabbed his flak jacket and started to drag him to the nearest courtyard that was bout 30 meters away from where he was. Now Mac is a very big guy, and heavy at that, so I was moving him a little bit at a time. I yelled to Burke to assist me in dragging Mac into the courtyard. Once we got him into the courtyard where there was a 6 foot wall surrounding us, I dropped my weapon and noticed that Mac's helmet was choking him. I unsnapped it and he started breathing and gasping for air. At that moment I felt like 10 million pounds off my chest, like I could breathe myself and I prayed.

235

The whole squad was in there now and the corpsman arrived. Doc Primera and I started to work on Mac trying to keeping him alive. Half the squad went in the house and cleared it, the other half stayed and secured the courtyard so we can work on Mac. Burke and Sgt Davidson started working on Mac's medivac to get him out of there. The whole time I'm yelling at Mac, "Yo man!! Talk to me! Tell me something! Tell me something about ur mom or dad maybe back home. At this point I have one arm under his head supporting it and plugging the exit wound and the other hand over his face plugging the face wound. Doc was taking his heart beat and checking his eyes when I noticed that Mac was choking on something. It sounded like he was snoring and choking at the same time, so I told Doc to grab one of the wounds so I can sweep his mouth for anything. Sure enough he was choking on phlegm and blood, plus I believe he had a dip of Copenhagen. haha! But as soon as I swept his mouth a second time to make sure I got everything he quickly turned his body around as if he was going to do a push up and clamped down on my finger. He was biting my finger and I yelled at the top of my lungs Mac dude ur biting my finger man, @#%* let go. Hahaha. SO he did.

Mac was able to understand us and communicate with us through sounds and movements but he couldn't talk or speak a sentence until our quick reaction force came. When they showed up, he started to talk about the sniper that shot him and how he wanted to kill him, that he was fine, to let him go, get the #%@! It was crazy, like u figure a man that just got shot in the head would be out of it or something else, but talking and telling us he's fine. hahaha So we loaded him up and sent him on his way as we prayed.

Now this is the good part, as soon as they left I was pissed, crying out of anger. I saw Mac's blood soaking the ground of that nasty @#%! place so I started to scoop up his blood and put it in my pocket cuz no American Marine or American person's blood should ever soak the dirt of Iraq. At least that's how I see things, I wouldn't want my blood on that @#%! place so I sure as hell ain't gonna let one of my guys blood stay there.

236

MARIO ANES RECEIVING THE NAVY AND MARINE
ACHIEVEMENT MEDAL

237

When we got back to base everyone started to pray in the platoon for Mac's health and his family. I couldn't sleep for about 4 days cuz every time I kept closing my eyes, I would see Mac's face the way it was and the blood, it was a sight I will never forget. So Mac was being prayed for, not only from his immediate family but us, his second family, too. We love that guy and wished he could of shared the memories over there with us but I'm glad things worked out the way they did, or else who knows what could of happened later on down the road.

Mack I love u man and this squad, platoon, company does, too. Take care

Mario

Oh yea who all was there, Sgt. Davidson, Cpl Anes, the rest are LCpl. Burke, Marchitell, Jones, Acosta, Keys, Landry, Doc and Checchia.

In December, 2007 Cpl. Anes was promoted to Sgt., and in January 2008, he received the Navy and Marine Achievement Medal & Certificate for his heroic and selfless acts which strongly contributed to John's survival. However, in my opinion, Mario's greatest reward, is knowing John is alive and well because of Mario's heroic actions. His second biggest reward is the undying love and appreciation of John, his family, friends and community. Without Mario, there would be no *My Miracle Marine*.

Footnote: In October of 2006 we learned the men of 2/3 Echo had killed the sniper who shot John. Two weeks after John was wounded, one of the men of 2/3 experienced a near miss sniper shot after which his unit immediately raced to cut the sniper off. Believing they had a line on the sniper's vehicle, a high speed chase ensued.

The vehicle wrecked and the suspects fled on foot. One of 2/3's gunners leapt from the gunners turret and pursued the sniper. The men of 2/3 shot and wounded the sniper, but he escaped. Later that night, our men found out where the wounded escapee lived and so, they raided his house where they learned he had already died. At the home, our men confiscated the M16A4 with ACOG and silencer used in the sniper incident.

Justice had been served.

238

Afterword

I n order to have our prayers answered, it is imperative that we believe and not doubt; however, this is not always easy when we are engulfed in life's trials and tribulations. I am convinced that my network of faithful, prayer partners played an integral part in the story of my miracle Marine.

In November of 2007, I needed to make the decision of whether *My Miracle Marine* was going to continue to be my dream, or whether it was going to be a reality. The time had come for us to invest the money needed for publication. So, on November 20th, during my prayer time, I prayed, "God, I need for You to show me *My Miracle Marine* is of You and not of me, because if it's not of You, I'm not going forward with it. I need You to give me a clear sign."

Routinely, during my morning prayer time, I read from a book called *Words of Wisdom*, which is a compilation of the Bible's books of Psalms and Proverbs divided into thirty-one days. By the end of each month, I've read both books in their entirety. On this day, the reading was Psalms 96:

239

Sing a new song to the Lord! Sing it everywhere around the world! Sing out His praises! Bless His name. Each day tell someone that He saves.

Publish His Glorious acts throughout the earth. Tell everyone about the amazing things He does. For the Lord is great beyond description and greatly to be praised.

"Got it!" I thought, as tears streamed down my face. It doesn't get much clearer than that! Without a doubt, *My Miracle Marine* was God's project, and I, the instrument.

240

As I progressed with writing *My Miracle Marine*, its purpose became more and more clear. What I felt God wanted people to learn from this book was:

1.) There is hope in God, as He is still in the miracle working business.
2.) Prayer really does work.
3.) There are no such things as coincidences.

As relayed in *My Miracle Marine*, God consistently blessed John, Carl and me with miraculous healings and happenstances. I believe part of the reason He blessed us in that way, was because I had consistently been obedient to what He has told me in His Word:

a.) I prayed and led prayer for John without ceasing from the time he was first deployed.

b.) I believed and did not doubt that John would be okay.

I believe God allowed John to be shot and saved, so that his story could be shared. And, I believe He chose me as the instrument for telling this story because:

a.) He knew I had no pride and wouldn't worry about what people thought. He knew I would give Him credit and boldly proclaim to the masses all of the miracles God had performed, no matter how small. I thank God for taking away my pride.

b.) He had given me a gift of communication with which I could easily convey His miracles via email. I thank God for giving me the gift of communication.

241

c.) He had given me a gift of faith, which I believe served as a witness to the   thousands of people connected to this story. I thank God for giving me the gift of faith.

d.) The combination of my faith, boldness and writing skills helped to teach people how to pray effectively.

Please do not take the above as bragging.

Finally, I want to give words of encouragement to those who have lost loved ones, whether it happened on the battlefields of Iraq or Afghanistan, or just the battlefields of life. I know I'm not the only praying

Mom. I know there are praying Moms all over the country who believed their sons or daughters would come home safely. Please be encouraged to know their dying is not the end all. You will see your loved ones in heaven. I truly believe, in the meantime, God has a valuable purpose for them and He is using them in a mighty way in the heavenly realm.

www.mymiraclemarine.com